♏ THE SCORPIO ENIGMA ♏

Cracking the Code.

ALSO BY JANE RIDDER-PATRICK

A Handbook of Medical Astrology
Shaping Your Future (Series of 12 titles)
Shaping Your Relationships (Series of 12 titles)

The Zodiac Code series

THE
SCORPIO
ENIGMA

Cracking the Code

23 October – 21 November

Jane Ridder-Patrick

MAINSTREAM
PUBLISHING

EDINBURGH AND LONDON

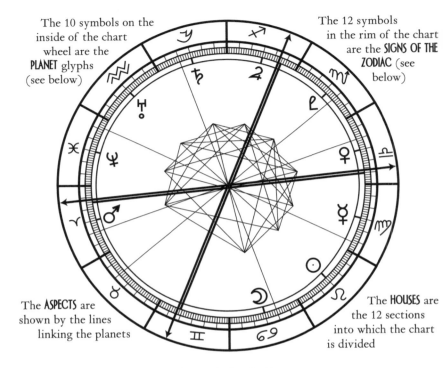

The 10 symbols on the inside of the chart wheel are the **PLANET** glyphs (see below)

The 12 symbols in the rim of the chart are the **SIGNS OF THE ZODIAC** (see below)

The **ASPECTS** are shown by the lines linking the planets

The **HOUSES** are the 12 sections into which the chart is divided

A Sample Birth Chart

Sign	Ruler	Sign	Ruler
Aries ♈	Mars ♂	Libra ♎	Venus ♀
Taurus ♉	Venus ♀	Scorpio ♏	Pluto ♇
Gemini ♊	Mercury ☿	Sagittarius ♐	Jupiter ♃
Cancer ♋	Moon ☽	Capricorn ♑	Saturn ♄
Leo ♌	Sun ☉	Aquarius ♒	Uranus ♅
Virgo ♍	Mercury ☿	Pisces ♓	Neptune ♆

In memory of my grandmother,
Isabella McNair

Reprinted 2009

First published in Great Britain in 2004 by
MAINSTREAM PUBLISHING COMPANY
(EDINBURGH) LTD
7 Albany Street
Edinburgh EH1 3UG

ISBN 9781840185324

A catalogue record for this book is available
from the British Library

Typeset in Allise and Van Dijck

Printed in Great Britain by
CPI Antony Rowe, Chippenham, SN14 6LH

Contents

ONE

The Truth of Astrology

MOST PEOPLE'S FIRST EXPERIENCE OF ASTROLOGY IS THROUGH newspapers and magazines. This is a mixed blessing for astrology's reputation – writing an astrology column to any degree of accuracy is a tough, many would say impossible, challenge. The astrologer has to try to say something meaningful about conditions that affect every single person belonging to the same sign, over a very short period of time, in a scant handful of words. The miracle is that some talented astrologers do manage to get across a tantalising whiff of the real thing and keep readers coming back for more of what most of us are hungry for – self-knowledge and reassurance about the future. The downside of the popularity of these columns is that many people think that all astrology is a branch of the entertainment industry and is limited to light-hearted fortune-telling. This is far from the truth.

What Astrology Can Offer
Serious astrology is one of the most sophisticated tools available to help us understand ourselves and the world

around us. It gives us a language and a framework to examine and describe – quite literally – *anything* under the Sun, from countries to companies, from money markets to medical matters. Its most common application, however, is in helping people to understand themselves better using their own unique birth charts. Astrology has two main functions. One is to describe the traits and tendencies of whatever it is that is being examined, whether this is a state, a software company or someone's psyche. The other is to give an astonishingly accurate timetable for important changes within that entity. In the chapters that follow, we'll be using astrology to investigate the psychology of the innermost part of your personality, taking a look at what drives, inspires and motivates you.

Astrology uses an ancient system of symbols to describe profound truths about the nature of life on earth, truths that cannot be weighed and measured, but ones we recognise nevertheless, and that touch and move us at a deep level. By linking mythology and mathematics, astrology bridges the gap between our inner lives and our outer experiences, between mind and matter, between poetry and science.

Fate and Free Will

Some people think that astrology is all about foretelling the future, the implication being that everything is predestined and that we have no say in how our lives take shape. None of that is true. We are far from being helpless victims of fate. Everything that happens to us at any given time is the result of past choices. These choices may have been our own, or made by other people. They could even have been made long ago before we, or even our grandparents, were born. It is not always possible to prevent processes that were set in motion in the past from coming to their logical conclusions as events that we then have to deal with. We are, however, all free to decide how to react to whatever is presented to us at every moment of our lives.

Your destiny is linked directly with your personality because the choices you make, consciously or unconsciously, depend largely on your own natural inclinations. It is these inclinations that psychological astrology describes. You can live out every single part of your chart in a constructive or a less constructive way. For instance, if you have Aries strong in your chart, action and initiative will play a major role in your life. It is your choice whether you express yourself aggressively or assertively, heroically or selfishly, and also whether you are the doer or the done-to. Making the right choices is important because every decision has consequences – and what you give out, sooner or later, you get back. If you don't know and understand yourself, you are 'fated' to act according to instinct and how your life experiences have conditioned you. By revealing how you are wired up temperamentally, astrology can highlight alternatives to blind knee-jerk reactions, which often make existing problems worse. This self-knowledge can allow you to make more informed free-will choices, and so help you create a better and more successful future for yourself.

Astrology and Prediction

Astrology cannot predict specific events based on your birth chart. That kind of prediction belongs to clairvoyance and divination. These specialities, when practised by gifted and responsible individuals, can give penetrating insights into events that are likely to happen in the future if matters proceed along their present course.

The real benefit of seeing into the future is that if we

don't like what could happen if we carry on the way we're going, we can take steps either to prevent it or to lessen its impact. Rarely is the future chiselled out in stone. There are many possible futures. What you feed with your attention grows. Using your birth chart, a competent astrologer can map out, for years in advance, major turning points, showing which areas of your life will be affected at these times and the kind of change that will be taking place. This information gives answers to the questions that most clients ask in one way or another: 'Why me, why this and why now?' If you accept responsibility for facing what needs to be done at the appropriate time, and doing it, you can change the course of your life for the better.

Astrology and the Soul

What is sometimes called the soul and its purpose is a mystery much more profound than astrology. Most of us have experienced 'chance' meetings and apparent 'tragedies' which have affected the direction of our entire lives. There is an intelligence at work that is infinitely wiser and more powerful than the will or wishes of our small, egocentric personalities. This force, whatever name we give it – Universal Wisdom, the Inner Guide, the Self, a guardian angel – steers us into exactly the right conditions for our souls' growth. Astrology can pinpoint the turning points in the course of your destiny and describe the equipment that you have at your disposal for serving, or resisting, the soul's purpose. That equipment is your personality.

Who Are You?

You are no doubt aware of your many good qualities as well as your rather more resistible ones that you might prefer to keep firmly under wraps. Maybe you have wondered why it is that one part of your personality seems to want to do one thing while another part is stubbornly intent on doing the exact opposite. Have you ever wished that you could crack the code that holds the secrets of what makes you – and significant others – behave in the complex way you do? The good news is that you can, with the help of your astrological birth chart, sometimes known as your horoscope.

Just as surely as your DNA identifies you and distinguishes you from everyone else, as well as encoding your peculiarities and potential, your birth chart reveals the unique 'DNA fingerprinting' of your personality. This may seem a staggering claim, but it is one that those who have experienced serious astrology will endorse, so let's take a closer look at what a birth chart is.

Your Birth Chart

Your birth chart is a simplified diagram of the positions of the planets, as seen from the place of your birth, at the moment you took your first independent breath. Critics have said that astrology is obviously nonsense because birth charts are drawn up as if the Sun and all the planets moved round the Earth.

We know in our minds that the Earth moves round the Sun, but that doesn't stop us seeing the Sun rise in the east in the morning and move across the sky to set in the west in the evening. This is an optical illusion. In the same way, we know (or at least most of us know) that we are not really the centre of the universe, but that doesn't stop us experiencing ourselves as being at the focal point of our own personal worlds. It is impossible to live life in any other way. It is the strength, not weakness, of astrology that it describes from your own unique viewpoint how you, as an individual, experience life.

Erecting Your Chart

To draw up a full birth chart you need three pieces of information – the date, time and place of your birth. With your birth date alone you can find the positions of all the planets (except sometimes the Moon) to a good enough degree of accuracy to reveal a great deal of important information about you. If you have the time and place of birth, too, an astrologer can calculate your Ascendant or Rising Sign and the houses of your chart – see below. The Ascendant is a bit like the front door of your personality and describes your general outlook on life. (If you know your Ascendant sign, you might like to read more about its characteristics in the book on that sign in this series.)

The diagram on page 6 shows what a birth chart looks like. Most people find it pretty daunting at first sight but it actually breaks down into only four basic units – the planets, the signs, the aspects and the houses.

The Planets

Below is a simple list of what the planets represent.

PLANET	REPRESENTS YOUR URGE TO
☉ The Sun	express your identity
☽ The Moon	feel nurtured and safe
☿ Mercury	make connections
♀ Venus	attract what you love
♂ Mars	assert your will
♃ Jupiter	find meaning in life
♄ Saturn	achieve your ambitions
♅ Uranus	challenge tradition
♆ Neptune	serve an ideal
♇ Pluto	eliminate, transform and survive

The planets represent the main psychological drives that every single one of us has. The exact way in which we express these drives is not fixed from birth but develops and evolves throughout our lives, both consciously and unconsciously. In this book we will be examining in detail four of these planets – your Sun, Moon, Mercury and Venus. These are the bodies that are right at the heart of our solar system. They correspond, in psychological astrology, to the core of your personality and represent how you express yourself, what motivates you emotionally, how you use your mind and what brings you pleasure.

The Signs

The signs your planets are in show how you tend to express your inner drives. For example, if your Mars is in the action sign of Aries, you will assert yourself pretty directly, pulling no punches. If your Venus is in secretive Scorpio, you will attract, and be attracted to, emotionally intense relationships. There is a summary of all of the signs on p. 128.

The Aspects

Aspects are important relationships between planets and whether your inner characteristics clash with or complement each other depends largely on whether or not they are in aspect and whether that aspect is an easy or a challenging one. In Chapter Six we'll be looking at some challenging aspects to the Sun.

The Houses

Your birth chart is divided into 12 slices, called houses, each of which is associated with a particular area of life, such as friendships, travel or home life. If, for example, you have your Uranus in the house of career, you are almost certainly a bit of a maverick at work. If you have your Neptune in the house of partnership, you are likely to idealise your husband, wife or business partner.

The Nature of Time

Your birth chart records a moment in time and space, like a still from a movie – the movie being the apparent movement of the planets round the earth. We all know that time is something that can be measured in precise units, which are always the same, like seconds, months and centuries. But if you stop to reflect for a moment, you'll also recognise that time doesn't always feel the same. Twenty minutes waiting for a bus on a cold, rainy day can seem like a miserable eternity, while the same amount of time spent with someone you love can pass in a flash. As Einstein would say – that's relativity.

There are times in history when something significant seems to be in the air, but even when nothing momentous is happening the quality of time shifts into different 'moods' from moment to moment. Your birth chart is impregnated with the qualities of the time when you were born. For example, people who were born in the mid-to-late 1960s, when society was undergoing major disruptive changes, carry those powerful energies within them and their personalities reflect, in many ways, the turmoil of those troubled and exciting times. Now, as adults, the choices that those individuals make, based on their own inner conflicts and compulsions, will help shape the future of society for better or worse. And so it goes on through the generations.

Seed Meets Soil

There is no such thing as a good or bad chart, nor is any one sign better or worse than another. There are simply 12 different, but equally important, life focuses. It's useful to keep in mind the fact that the chart of each one of us is made up of all the signs of the zodiac. This means that we'll act out, or experience, *every* sign somewhere in our lives. It is true, however, that some individual charts are more challenging than others; but the greater the challenge, the greater the potential for achievement and self-understanding.

In gardening terms, your chart is a bit like the picture on a seed packet. It shows what you could become. If the seeds are of poppies, there's no way you'll get petunias, but external conditions will affect how they grow. With healthy soil, a friendly climate and green-fingered gardeners, the plants have an excellent chance of flourishing. With poor soil, a harsh climate or constant neglect, the seeds will be forced to struggle. This is not always a disadvantage. They can become hardy and adapt, finding new and creative ways of evolving and thriving under more extreme conditions than the plant that was well cared for. It's the same with your chart. The environment you were raised in may have been friendly or hostile to your nature and it will have done much to shape your life until now. Using the insights of astrology to affirm who you are, you can, as an adult, provide your own ideal conditions, become your own best gardener and live out more fully – and successfully – your own highest potential.

TWO

The Symbolism of Scorpio

M WE CAN LEARN A GREAT DEAL ABOUT SCORPIO BY LOOKING at the symbolism and the myths and legends associated with it. These carry more information than plain facts alone and hint at the deeper meanings and significance of the sign.

Shaped like the letter M with the final stroke flicked up and barbed at the end, the Scorpio glyph has been interpreted in many ways over the years. It is said to represent a scorpion whose venomous tail is capable of stinging to death anything that threatens. It has been seen, too, as the coils of a serpent with its head raised, poised to strike. Both of these images refer to the scorpionic vigilance against predators and the ability to defend vigorously if attacked. Openly phallic, the glyph also represents the potent male member, ready for action, showing Scorpio's close connection with sex, desire and power.

Scorpio the Scorpion – and Other Creatures
The symbols of Scorpio are the scorpion, the serpent and the eagle. These correspond to the three levels of development

that Scorpios can pass through. The scorpion is associated with darkness and destruction, as well as death and rebirth. It operates at the level of instinctual survival. The scorpion is a shy creature that minds its own business and only attacks if thwarted or provoked. It will then move in for the kill, no matter how big the enemy. When cornered, a scorpion will sting itself to death rather than surrender, just like some Scorpios whose pride and stubborn refusal to tolerate defeat can be their undoing. The only remedy against its sting was believed to be an oil it carries inside itself, showing that Scorpios have within them the means of their own salvation. Interestingly, at the moment a new remedy for cancer is being developed by scientists from scorpion venom which, unlike chemotherapy, tracks down and destroys only malignant cells.

Next comes the serpent, which, as told in the Bible, successfully tempted Eve to eat the forbidden fruit of the tree of knowledge of good and evil. This led to the loss of innocence and the expulsion of Adam and Eve from the Garden of Eden. The symbolism of the serpent is strangely ambivalent: in some contexts and cultures it represents evil, guile, death and sexuality, and in others it is associated with intuitive wisdom, fertility, birth and healing. Most Scorpios are fascinated by the mysteries of life, death and sex and are often attracted to the occult and to investigating areas that other people consider taboo. The serpent has to shed and renew its old skin periodically to allow it to grow. Because of this, it was thought to be immortal. The lives of Scorpios often include critical stages of shedding the past, with one phase coming to a complete end and a new one beginning. The serpent is also linked with kundalini energy, energy that lies coiled in the root chakra, ready to rise to the crown when the person has matured enough to use the life force responsibly and wisely. Called up prematurely, it tends to destroy – just like the intense power that Scorpios have at their disposal, to heal or to harm.

Finally, there is the eagle that soars high above worldly temptations. The eagle symbolises spiritual power and the will and courage to overcome the powers of darkness and ascend into the radiant light of truth and love. It is often shown grappling with, and conquering, the serpent, which in this context represents the seductions of desire. The eagle with the serpent in its claws or beak is also a symbol of the union of intellect and instinct, and of spiritual and worldly power, that some Scorpios can and do achieve. A variation of the eagle theme is the phoenix, a mythical bird which burnt itself on a funeral pyre and then rose from the ashes to live through another cycle, echoing the tendency of Scorpios to have one life situation end completely, followed by a resurrection when they reinvent themselves.

The eagle is the symbol of St John the Evangelist, who is said to have understood the mysteries of creation and evolution, which he recorded in the Book of Revelation. He was the only disciple not to desert Jesus at his death, but stood loyally at the foot of the cross, just as Scorpios rarely bale out just because the going gets tough. He is shown with a chalice containing a serpent, referring to his reputation for rendering poison harmless, which is why he is the patron saint against poisoning. St John is sometimes depicted in a cauldron of boiling oil, into which he was thrown because of his faith, but he stepped out unharmed. These images are as extreme as the sign itself and many Scorpios, like St John, come out of extreme situations safe, and even transformed and empowered.

The Ruler of Scorpio

Scorpio is ruled, or associated with, two very different planets – Mars and Pluto. Mars, the god of war, is the traditional ruler while the modern ruler, Pluto, planet of death and transformation, was only discovered in 1930. In mythology Pluto, also known as Hades, was the god of the Underworld, the place of the dead. He abducted and raped Persephone, goddess of the spring, wrenching her away from her overprotective mother, Demeter. Although he stole her innocence forcibly, they later married and she grew into a mature woman and a self-assured queen. There are some familiar Scorpio themes here . . . betrayal, loss of naivety, abuse of power, brushes with life's underworld – and out of evil and darkness, the emergence of new life.

The Season of Scorpio

During Scorpio's month, in the northern hemisphere, the trees are almost bare and the nights draw in, heralding the cold and darkness to come. Animals are preparing for hibernation while the first chill of winter is felt. The year is dying as the forces of life are overtaken by death and plant life retreats into its roots and seeds. All of this is a vital part of the cycle of life. The earth rests, holding in its depths the seeds of next spring's splendour and the rotting vegetation transforms slowly into rich, sweet, life-giving soil. Human activities change and energy which was directed outward is now turned to inner resources. At this time, throughout the world, there are feasts in remembrance of the dead. The old fire festival of Samhain, based on an earlier Druid sacred day, falls in the sign of Scorpio and is still celebrated today as Hallowe'en. Most significantly, it was the Celtic New Year, in recognition of the fact that death and birth are irrevocably linked and that new life has its beginnings, quietly and secretly, in the dark. Scorpio is the first sign that moves from being purely concerned with outer worldly affairs. All of the signs that follow on from Scorpio have part of their focus at least on the otherworldly.

THREE

The Heart of the Sun

⊙ THE GLYPH FOR THE SUN IS A PERFECT CIRCLE WITH A DOT in the centre and symbolises our dual nature – earthly and eternal. The circle stands for the boundary of the personality, which distinguishes and separates each individual from every other individual, for it is our differences from other people that make us unique, not our similarities. The dot in the centre indicates the mysterious 'divine spark' within us and the potential for becoming conscious of who we truly are, where we have come from and what we may become.

The Meaning of the Sun

Each of your planets represents a different strand of your personality. The Sun is often reckoned to be the most important factor of your whole birth chart. It describes your sense of identity, and the sign that the Sun was in when you were born, your Sun sign, along with its house position and any aspects to other planets, shows how you express and develop that identity.

Your Role in Life

Each of the signs is associated with certain roles that can be played in an infinite number of ways. Take one of the roles of Aries, which is the warrior. A warrior can cover anything from Attila the Hun, who devastated vast stretches of Europe with his deliberate violence, to an eco-warrior, battling to save the environment. The role, warrior, is the same; the motivation and actions are totally different. You can live out every part of your personality in four main ways – as creator, destroyer, onlooker or victim. How you act depends on who you choose to be from the endless variations possible from the symbolism of each of your planets, but most particularly your Sun. And you do have a choice; not all Geminis are irresponsible space cadets nor is every Scorpio a sex-crazed sadist. This book aims to paint a picture of what some of your choices might be and show what choices, conscious or unconscious, some well-known people of your sign have made.

Your upbringing will have helped shape what you believe about yourself and out of those beliefs comes, automatically, behaviour to match. For example, if you believe you are a victim, you will behave like one and the world will happily oblige by victimising you. If you see yourself as a carer, life will present you with plenty to care for – and often to care about, too. If you identify yourself as an adventurer, you'll spot opportunities at every corner. If you're a winner, then you'll tend to succeed. Shift the way that you see yourself and your whole world shifts, too.

Your Vocation

Your Sun describes your major life focus. This is not always a career. As the poet Milton said: 'They also serve who only stand and wait.' It is impossible to tell from your Sun sign exactly what your calling is – there are people of all signs occupied in practically every area of life. What is important is not so much *what* you do, but the way that you do it and it is this – how you express yourself – that your Sun describes. If you spend most of your time working at an occupation or living in a situation where you can't give expression to the qualities of your Sun, or which forces you to go against the grain of your Sun's natural inclinations, then you're likely to live a life of quiet, or possibly even noisy, desperation.

On Whose Authority

Your personality, which your birth chart maps, is like a sensitive instrument that will resonate only to certain frequencies – those that are similar to its own. Your Sun shows the kind of authority that will strike a chord with you, either positively or negatively, because it is in harmony with yours. It can show how you relate to people in authority, especially your father. (It is the Moon that usually shows the relationship with your mother and home.) In adult life it can throw light onto the types of bosses you are likely to come across, and also how you could react to them. It is a major part of the maturing process to take responsibility for expressing your own authority wisely. When you do so, many of your problems with external authorities diminish or even disappear.

In a woman's chart the Sun can also describe the kind of husband she chooses. This is partly because, traditionally, a husband had legal authority over his wife. It is also because, especially in the early years of a marriage, many women choose to pour their energies into homemaking and supporting their husbands' work in the world, rather than their own, and so his career becomes her career. As a

Scorpio, you may find that your father, boss or husband shows either the positive or negative traits of Scorpio or, as is usually the case, a mixture of both – determined, protective and dignified or suspicious, controlling and intimidating.

Born on the Cusp

If you were born near the beginning or end of Scorpio, you may know that your birthday falls on the cusp, or meeting point, of two signs. The Sun, however, can only be in one sign or the other. You can find out for sure which sign your Sun is in by checking the tables on pp. 98–9.

FOUR

The Drama of Being a Scorpio

EACH SIGN IS ASSOCIATED WITH A CLUSTER OF ROLES THAT HAVE their own core drama or storyline. Being born is a bit like arriving in the middle of an ongoing play and slipping into a certain part. How we play our characters is powerfully shaped in early life by having to respond to the input of the other actors around us – the people that make up our families and communities. As the play of our lives unfolds, we usually become aware that there are themes which tend to repeat themselves. We may ask ourselves questions like 'Why do I always end up with all the work / caught up in fights / with partners who mistreat me / in dead-end jobs / successful but unhappy . . .?' or whatever. Interestingly, I've found that people are less likely to question the wonderful things that happen to them again and again.

The good news is that once we recognise the way we have been playing our roles, we can then use our free-will choice to do some creative re-scripting, using the same character in more constructive scenarios. Even better news is that if we change, the other people in our dramas have got to make some alterations, too. If you refuse to respond to the same old cues in the customary ways, they are going to have to get creative, too.

A key role of Scorpio is the survivor. Survivors find themselves in dangerous, and often extreme, situations where life, love, livelihood, sanity, self-esteem or anything which seems essential to their own, or loved ones', existence is under threat. The stakes are high. Against the odds, they are able to live through the experience and frequently even grow stronger in the process. The menace can come from outside of themselves, in the form of other people or events, or from their own bodies, thoughts or emotions. Usually, what threatens is, or is believed to be, much more powerful than the person who is threatened — and is often partly hidden or unknown.

Attack can come from anywhere, and at any time, so the survivor must be prepared for all eventualities. To succeed, he or she needs to be constantly vigilant and, looking beyond and behind surface appearances, be super-sensitive to anything that might possibly signal that danger is lurking just round the corner. Everything has to be treated as guilty until proven innocent; safety lies in taking precautions and in investigating closely anything remotely suspicious. As it is important not to draw attention to themselves, in case they could be marked out as prey, survivors tend to be still and secretive, keeping their heads down, maintaining a low profile. Their tightly reined-in energy of watchfulness and pent-up aggression creates a powerful emotional field that is almost palpable, and can often intimidate predators. Most survivors, however, stay on the defensive and don't launch attacks unless attacked first, or believing an attack is imminent. If cornered, they can resort to formidable cunning and stealth to escape. But when their backs are truly against the wall, and all escape routes are barred, those running on survival energy are ruthless and fight to the last, often preferring to destroy themselves rather than be captured or crushed by the opponent.

Some survivors focus solely on themselves and, cruelly disregarding others, become predators, extorting whatever they need from wherever and whomever it's available. Others, despite danger and self-deprivation, show the highest qualities of human love, courage and endurance by tending to, and protecting, others. Nature ensures that the sex drive is strong when survival is at risk, to safeguard the continuation of the species. It also functions as a short-term, but effective, tension reliever.

When the danger period is over, survivors can be haunted by memories of the past. They often carry deep emotional scars, as well as a burning resentment, and may demand retribution to regain some sense of power. They'll then track their former tormentors down by fair means or foul, no matter how long it takes, to extract their just revenge. Others are equally determined that no one else should have to experience the fear, and possibly degradation, that they have gone through. So they become powerful champions and protectors of the vulnerable and are ready to confront and transform the people, force or illness that threatened them.

Other Scorpio roles are the investigator, defender, scapegoat, researcher, eliminator, recycler, midwife, healer, whistle-blower and sorcerer or hypnotist, all of which deal with life, death, mysteries, power and transformation in various different guises.

How you choose to see your role will determine your behaviour. The following chapter describes some typical Scorpio behaviour. Remember, though, that there is no such thing as a person who is all Scorpio and nothing but Scorpio. You are much more complicated than that and other parts of your chart will modify, or may even seem to contradict, the single, but central, strand of your personality which is your Sun sign. These other sides of your nature will add colour and contrast and may restrict or reinforce your basic Scorpio identity. They won't, however, cancel out the challenges you face as a Scorpio.

FIVE

The Scorpio Temperament

SUPERFICIAL APPEARANCES DON'T FOOL YOU. BECAUSE YOU'RE SO aware of life's dark underbelly, watchfulness is, for you, just plain common sense. Your sensitive emotional radar scans the environment constantly, monitoring it for the slightest whiff of danger or deviousness. This means you register deceit and hypocrisy instantly and can smell a rat a mile away. Anything suspicious sets off powerful bodily reactions, leaving you feeling as if you've been hit in the solar plexus or that your guts are turning to jelly. Like a seasoned poker player, you carefully conceal what's going on behind an inscrutable exterior. Few would guess that beneath your millpond-smooth surface run deep, dark rivers of emotion, turbulent with cross-currents.

Sneaking Suspicions

You're normally right about who can be trusted and who can't, but sometimes your suspicions get out of hand. This usually happens when old memories are triggered off and, with them, instinctive reactions to events that have little connection with the present moment. All emotionally charged experiences leave you with indelible marks but a vital key to your happiness is learning to interpret your moods and feelings accurately. Distinguishing between genuine responses to what is happening in the here and now, and flashbacks from the past, can mean the difference between being incapacitated by paranoia and developing a finely tuned emotional intelligence that could give you formidable advantages in all situations.

The Courage to Confront

Some Scorpios live in constant fear of being blamed, attacked or scapegoated. To protect themselves, they'll shrink back from the foreground, trying to become invisible and to take up as little space as possible. They'll also do every task with a scrupulousness that borders on the obsessive. Almost unrecognisable as Scorpios, they can appear so fragile that a puff of wind would blow them away, but push them too far and their true mettle will show. Your challenge as a Scorpio is to confront your worst fears. That requires courage and a steely will. Fortunately, you possess both of these qualities in abundance. In the film *The Wizard of Oz*, the terrifying wizard is finally discovered to be only a rather pathetic old man behind a curtain, cranking up a machine to create illusions. That's the freedom that comes when you stop barricading yourself in against your nightmares and dare to look at what is really going on. Once you've done so, you'll realise that there's rarely anything to fear but fear itself – and you'll eliminate the terrorising power of the wicked wizard of your imagination.

Weapons of War

If, however, you are genuinely under threat, or there is trouble to be tackled, you have some fearsome weapons at your disposal. You may believe that attack is the best form of defence — though not necessarily the open and up-front variety. You might prefer to undermine the opposition with insinuations and unspoken threats or promises, or by manufacturing an atmosphere heavily laced with menace and intimidation. Manipulating and manoeuvring situations to your own advantage is easy because of your instinctive understanding of other people's desires and vulnerabilities. If it's clear that you're going to be defeated, you won't surrender meekly. As one Scorpio told me: 'If I'm going down, I'm not going alone. I'm taking everyone and everything down with me.' That Armageddon stance could mean that, out of pride and spite, you could be tempted to destroy the life you've so painstakingly built up for yourself.

Life on the Edge

Being a Scorpio means that you have almost certainly had intense or life-changing encounters with sex, death, secrets, corruption or the betrayal of trust. The Icelandic singer Björk was stalked by a mentally ill man who tried to kill her by sending her a hollowed-out book filled with explosives. He committed suicide shortly afterwards. Some Scorpios become sucked into webs of intrigue and double-dealing. You may have known evil, coercion, insanity or abuse, or had sexual attentions, wanted or unwanted, forced upon you. It was an obsession with Scorpio actress Jodie Foster that John Hinckley claimed was behind his attempt to assassinate the US president Ronald Reagan. You could have been at the mercy of someone, or circumstances, where you felt out of control — or you may know what it is like to be overwhelmed by your own compulsions, desire for power or capacity for destruction. It may be your work that takes you into these areas. These difficult experiences are

31

the raw materials of your life. Evil, by its presence, allows us to know and to choose to practise good. Without it, the best in you could never be drawn out and tested.

Courage in Adversity

The dignified and heroic way you cope with trouble and trauma is awesome. With your powerful compassion and sympathy for the suffering, especially for those whose survival is threatened, you can transform pain and sorrow into love and redemption. One of the Rev. Chad Varah's first duties as a young vicar in 1936 was to bury a 14-year-old girl who had killed herself when her periods started, because she thought she had an incurable disease. This affected him so deeply that, to fight such dangerous and widespread ignorance, he started teaching sex education in youth clubs, an act of great courage as the subject was then virtually taboo. He went on to found The Samaritans, the telephone counselling service for those who are suicidal or despairing. My own grandmother, who had both her Sun and Moon in Scorpio, brought up eight children, for a time single-handedly, in dire poverty, but unreservedly gave of herself to others in need. She was the unofficial midwife in her area and once, while helping a neighbour give birth, went into labour herself, but insisted on staying on until the other woman's baby was safely delivered.

Forbidden Fruits

Taboo topics fascinate you. You can be repelled, yet compelled, by pornography, stories of horror and other murkier aspects of the human experience. Prohibiting a Scorpio from doing or knowing something is to ensure that they'll find a way to do so. The writer Harold Nicolson was only eight years old when the prime minister of Bulgaria, where he was living at the time, was assassinated and in his attempt to save himself, had his fingers chopped off. His widow pickled these in alcohol and put them in her window for supporters to honour. Little Harold was strictly forbidden to view the relics but tricked his nurse into taking him, where he ogled in wide-eyed fascination. The nurse had hysterics and Harold was punished for being heartless and disgusting. In fact, he was only following his Scorpionic compulsion to look unflinchingly at the unvarnished truth. Another young Scorpio I know got into serious trouble for crawling under a nun's long skirts, desperate to know what was concealed in their darkness.

Secrets and Lies

You are fond of secrets and guard your own closely. Even if you have nothing at all to hide, you like to keep your personal affairs strictly private. You are skilled at erecting smokescreens, being indirect, or even deliberately misleading, to put any snoopers off your track. This reticence can give you an aura of mystery and enigma. You're not averse, though, to keeping tabs on what's going on in the lives of others. You love to probe into people's secrets and draw out confessions. Once your suspicions are aroused that someone is lying or withholding information, you won't rest until you've got to the bottom of what is really going on. If asked your opinion, especially if you feel your questioner is being naive or dodging the issue, your analysis of the situation can be brutally frank. Sometimes your insights can be a healing relief, as you'll dare to dish the dirt that others sweep under the carpet. Sometimes, though, it helps to remember that not everyone needs to eyeball the facts like you do and that, while the truth will set us free, if delivered too bluntly, it can do lasting damage, too.

Death

Scorpios are natural mystics, acutely aware that there is to life than the mundane superficialities of my life. The processes involved in the creation and destruction of life fascinate you, making you curious about sex, birth and death. Some are terrified, yet mesmerised, by death, worried that it equals annihilation – a possibility more frightening than death itself. Others believe in reincarnation, or an afterlife, and may be drawn to investigate this. There is a saying that a true warrior is one who has faced his own death. Paradoxically – and there is so much that is paradoxical about Scorpio – it is your intense desire to live forever, and your acute awareness of the presence of death in life, that makes you so vibrantly alive.

Nice and Nasty

Like the little girl in Longfellow's poem, who had a little curl right in the middle of her forehead, when you are good you are very, very good, but when you are bad . . . you are horrid. If you feel insecure, you can attack indiscriminately with spiteful little cruelties that hurt deeply, for you know exactly where and how to strike to inflict maximum damage. It's hard for you, then, to give wholehearted positive feedback and you'll withhold, or damn with faint praise, so as not to give your power away. You are also susceptible to bile-bitter attacks of envy where you want to, and sometimes do, destroy what you so passionately desire just because someone else has it. You may know the temptation to prey on, or exploit, the vulnerable. This primitive side of Scorpio can be as distressing to you as it is to others, but if harnessed for civilised ends, is a source of strength, as the following story suggests. Once, when the Buddha came to a village to teach, a snake said that, more than anything, it wanted to become his disciple. The Buddha agreed, provided the snake proved its sincerity by not biting anyone by his next annual visit. A year later Buddha arrived to find a battered and woeful serpent, weeping that it so wanted to be good, but since it had given up biting, people just trampled all over it. The Buddha smiled compassionately and said that he had told it not to bite, but hadn't forbidden it to hiss . . . Interestingly, many Scorpios do seem to hiss when they're angry.

Revenge is Sweet

You hate being told what to do and if anyone tries to push you around, you'll dig in your heels and act perversely, out of pure spite. If you've been hurt, attacked, disempowered or taken advantage of, you'll never forget it and itch to retaliate. You may well forgive (possibly . . .) but forgetting you regard as senseless, as that just leaves you wide open to being injured again. You'll rarely hold a grudge, though, if someone has damaged you accidentally and is genuinely sorry. They didn't, after all, do it on purpose. You have a long memory, too, for kindliness shown to you, which you'll return with loyalty and generosity. Your strong sense of justice is of the Old Testament variety; turning the other cheek has little appeal – an eye for an eye is more your style. You like to give wrongdoers a taste of their own medicine, letting them know what it feels like and warning them not to mess with you again. Usually you'll be satisfied with giving as good as you got and no more. But some Scorpios are vindictive and plot revenge for years, biding their time and moving in remorselessly for total destruction when the conditions are right.

From Hell to Eternity

The heart of Scorpio is a battleground between the forces of good and evil. Are you a Dark Lord or do you side with the Fellowship of the Ring? Do you choose to indulge your desire for worldly power and the gratification of the baser instincts, or do you dedicate your will to follow the path of Truth and Love? The temptations to cheat and think you'll get away with it are enormous. Your task is to wrestle with powerful desires, fiendish pride and the capacity for evil, both your own and those of others. At root, it's the battle for your own soul and winning that battle will cost – and give you – not less than everything. Robert Louis Stevenson, a Scorpio himself, described this archetypal struggle in *Dr Jekyll and Mr Hyde*, the tale of a man torn apart, and destroyed, by the conflict between decency and depravity. Some Scorpios need to follow the left-hand path until they reach rock bottom, but once the decision is made to turn to the light, their ability to transform themselves radically and make amends is nothing short of miraculous.

Caution: Scorpio at Work

With your phenomenal will, thoroughness, laser-like focus and seemingly superhuman endurance, you are capable of achieving just about anything you set your heart and mind on. You enjoy operating in stealth mode and often work best when you are slightly on the defensive, trying to outwit and keep one step ahead of your opponents. Politics may suit you well; there have been more Scorpio US presidents than those of any other sign, apart from Aquarius. It's not just money or success that motivates you, although you're certainly not averse to accumulating either. It's not even power, though that's attractive, too. You're much more interested in solving the mystery of who you are and what life is about in the process of achieving your goals.

Doing the Dirty Work

You'll do whatever it takes to achieve your ambitions. You know the price of success and are willing to pay it in full. Nothing's too tough for you to handle and you're usually prepared to do even the unpleasant jobs, both emotional and physical, that everyone else avoids. You expect others to pull their weight, though, and Scorpio bosses usually have teams of loyal, hardworking and trustworthy employees, because anybody unsuitable is eliminated quickly and efficiently.

Digging Deep

Your love of the hidden makes you a skilled investigator and an in-depth researcher. Marie Curie worked in gruelling conditions for years on several tons of raw materials to isolate just one tenth of a gram of radium for her Nobel Prize-winning work on X-rays. Michel Gauquelin was a French psychologist and statistician who risked his reputation, and was vilified, because of his impeccable research into the academically taboo area of astrology and – worse – showing that there is indeed a correlation between the planets and personality. Careers dealing with security could appeal, like the police or prison service, military intelligence or surveillance work.

Healing Power

Your deep empathy with other people's suffering and emotional darkness often comes from having experienced these things yourself. This can draw you towards psychology, hypnosis and psychotherapy, all of which try to get to the root cause of emotional problems and to eliminate them. Many excellent doctors and surgeons are Scorpios, as they have what it takes to inflict pain in order to heal or cut out what's dead, rotten or poisonous in the body. Among them are Christiaan Barnard, who pioneered human heart transplants, and Jonas Salk, who developed the polio vaccine, which practically eradicated the disease from the USA within 15 years.

The Phoenix Effect

Recycling and restoration is another option, ranging from garbage collector or sewage worker to the antiques trade. Anything to do with birth, death or transformation may also appeal, such as working as a midwife, undertaker, hospice carer or makeover artist. Scorpio writers and actors tend to be preoccupied with the Scorpionic themes of life and death, good and evil, decay, corruption and transformation.

Scorpio and Health

Scorpio rules the reproductive system and all of the organs and channels of elimination, including the large bowel, bladder and even the nose and sweat glands. Many of your health problems – should you have any at all – are likely to be focused on these areas. Common ailments include piles, fistulas, hernias, constipation and abscesses. Menstrual disorders for women, especially heavy periods and PMS, are often accompanied by throat symptoms, and in men prostate problems may put in an appearance. Psychologically, these are often related to issues of money, control and mortality, as well as suppressed rage, and if these issues are addressed the symptoms could well be alleviated.

Fighting Fit

Scorpios are seldom ill, but when you are it's often serious. However, more than any other sign, you possess formidable recuperative powers and many Scorpios have brought themselves back from the brink by willpower and sheer survival instinct. Part of the cure is often a prolonged rest to recharge your batteries, especially if, like many Scorpios, you have, with your intensity and determination, damaged your body by driving it too hard, burning the candle at both ends. A radical change of attitude can help, too, eliminating any bitter resentments and hatreds that are eating away at you.

Lightening Up

Your tendency to plot and brood, especially over old emotional sores, can develop into free-floating anxiety and black depressions. When feeling vulnerable, you can get caught on a hamster wheel of self-absorption, your moods lurching between cold cynicism and agonised despair. Obsessive thoughts can haunt and torment you, especially if you try to avoid looking at difficult aspects of yourself. Once you decide to confront your problems squarely, without blame or judgement either of yourself or others, you'll summon up the courage and insight to find a solution, no matter what the cost. You'll then be in a position to inspire and heal others who have experienced the same darkness.

Fatal Attractions

Trust doesn't come easily to you. Despite your voracious desire for relationship, you are cautious about letting others into your intimate space. You are looking for a deep connection where your soul is touched and there is no hypocrisy or secrecy. So you'll carefully watch those you're attracted to. If you are insecure, you may try to make them jealous, or expose them to sexual or financial temptation, to see if they resist. Extremes are your speciality and you don't like compromises. You are either fully in or fully out of a relationship. Passion is what drives you and superficial relationships are simply not your style. Losing yourself entirely in and through another is what makes you feel most fully alive. If you desire someone, you'll go through hell and high water to possess him or her, but if it's clear they're not interested, you'll cut them out of your life as if they'd never existed.

Control Freak

Love makes you vulnerable, as it could expose you to your worst nightmare – abandonment. So you'll try to stay in control but, taken too far, this can prevent you from having what you value above all else – honest emotional intimacy and a close, stable relationship. A strong, intuitive partner who isn't fooled or intimidated by your power games is ideal for you. Your fierce possessiveness and insane jealousy, which you'll often cover up by seeming cool or disdainful, can make you primitive about protecting what you see as yours. Your intense pride may stop you admitting that your partner has hurt you – or apologising if you're the one who has wounded. Fights are common in some Scorpio relationships which thrive on high-tension dramas and passionate reconciliations. Think of the roller-coaster marriages of Scorpio Richard Burton and Elizabeth Taylor, whose Moon is in Scorpio.

Loyal to the End

Once you've made a commitment, you're capable of enduring love, deep compassion and unshakeable loyalty.

Even if your marriage is fit for the scrapheap and you're completely miserable, you'll tend to hang on tightly, trying to make it work. You'll only leave if you find another emotionally secure relationship to move into or if you've finally, finally had enough. Then it's over. Full stop. If your partner tries to leave, the chances are you won't be sweet and civilised about it.

Scorpionic Sex

Sex means much more to you than the friction of two skins. It has a transcendent charge which is more to do with the soul's longing than that of the body. Through it, you can both lose and find yourself at the same time. It's often the only way you'll allow yourself to experience the bliss of surrender. Part of you craves to be totally consumed and enslaved by deep emotional passion, while another part fears it. Your sexuality can be driven by obsessions and compulsions, and is sometimes tinged with sado-masochism and power games. Some Scorpios avoid the highly-charged emotional issues that sex produces by turning workaholic, using their powerful libidos to drive their careers. Others abstain with gritted teeth. One thing's certain, you're never neutral about sex and can be a superb lover – tender, passionate and fully present.

SIX

Aspects of the Sun

PLANETS, JUST LIKE PEOPLE, CAN HAVE IMPORTANT RELATIONSHIPS with each other. These relationships are called aspects. Aspects to your Sun from any other planet can influence your personality markedly. The most powerful effects come with those from the slower-moving planets — Saturn, Uranus, Neptune or Pluto. Sometimes they can alter your ideas about yourself and your behaviour patterns so much that you may not feel at all typical of your sign in certain areas of your life.

Check if your birth date and year appear in the various sections below to find out if one or more of these planets was aspecting the Sun when you were born. Only the so-called challenging aspects have been included. These are formed when the planets are together, opposite or at right angles to each other in the sky.

Unfortunately, because space is restricted, other aspects have been left out, although they have similar effects to those described below and, for the same reason, a few dates will inevitably have been missed out, too. (You can find out for sure whether or not your Sun is aspected at my website

42

www.janeridderpatrick.com) If your Sun has no aspects to
Saturn, Uranus, Neptune or Pluto, you're more likely to be
a typical Scorpio.

Some well-known Scorpios with challenging aspects to
their Suns appear below. You can find more in the birthday
section at the end of the book.

Sun in Scorpio in Aspect with Saturn

If you were born between 1953 and 1956 or 1983 and 1985,
whether or not your birthday is listed below, you are likely
to feel the influence of Saturn on your Sun.

23 October–1 November in: 1932–3, 1940, 1946, 1953, 1962, 1969,
1975, 1982–3, 1991 and 1998
2–11 November in: 1933–4, 1940, 1947, 1954, 1963, 1970, 1976,
1984, 1992 and 1999
12–22 November in: 1934–5, 1941, 1948, 1955–6, 1964, 1971, 1977,
1984–5 and 1993

| Sarah Bernhardt | Richard Burton | John Cleese |
| Captain James Cook | Calista Flockhart | Sylvia Plath |

Scorpionic energy is, at the best of times, brooding and
introspective. Add Saturn and you have the extra dimension
of self-doubt and feelings of inadequacy to torture yourself
with, which, unchecked, can lead to depression, as it did for
the poet Sylvia Plath. Saturn can be a harsh inner critic,
drip-feeding discouragement. Whenever you accuse
yourself or others with words like 'shouldn't', 'ought',
'must', 'can't' or similar, Saturn is at work. See if you can
identify whose voice it is. Usually Saturn's messages are
wagging-finger commands from childhood and you may be
able to recall times when you were made to feel not good
enough and crushed. If you still believe, as an adult, that

you are a victim of authority figures 'out there' who are judging you and holding you back, you can become stubbornly uncooperative and overreact to criticism. Not surprisingly, those same authorities are likely to be somewhat reluctant to help, promote or recognise you and the vicious cycle can go on, with you digging yourself ever more deeply into a resentful rut.

It doesn't have to be like this. Saturn's agenda is to give form to whatever it touches. With the Sun, it goads you on to prove yourself, to make something of your life and to become a person of substance or a recognised authority within your profession or community. If you take time to identify your own authentic ambitions – not what you believe will bring approval from others and safety for yourself – and, accepting life's limitations gracefully, work steadily towards achieving them, you'll find that Saturn can be a loyal friend, his promptings keeping you on course to achieve the much-deserved success that is well within your reach.

Sun in Scorpio in Aspect with Uranus
If you were born between 1975 and 1980, whether or not your birthday is listed below, you are likely to feel the influence of Uranus on your Sun.

23 October–1 November in: 1934–7, 1955–7 and 1974–7
2–11 November in: 1937–40, 1957–9 and 1977–80
12–22 November in: 1940–41, 1959–61 and 1979–81

| Linda Evans | Jodie Foster | Indira Gandhi |
| Bill Gates | René Magritte | Jonathan Ross |

Uranus wants to change the system. Depending on how aware you are, you could either be a knee-jerk rebel who reflexly contradicts in word or actions whatever are normal or standard procedures, or you could use your powers more creatively. Your career or your relationships are likely to be remarkable or different in some way, either because you are way ahead of the field or because you are such a non-conformist – or just a bit of an oddball. Whatever else you are, you're unlikely to be dull or run-of-the-mill. You've a way of looking at the world that is different, though not necessarily as odd as that of the surrealist artist Magritte, who painted everyday scenes in unlikely combinations. One of his best-known paintings is of a man in a hat looking in a mirror at the back of the head of a man in a hat.

Bill Gates spearheaded and revolutionised the world of computing and succeeded spectacularly in linking his ingenuity with the Scorpionic love of power. You need plenty of new and varied tasks and challenges to work on or you'll start to feel caged. Be careful, though, not to sabotage your own achievements when success comes, by abruptly moving on because you are bored or restless.

Your father may have been unusual in some way and, especially if you are a woman, a conventional home situation may be hard to tolerate, as you need so much freedom. Sun with Uranus makes you an agent for change and at its best you can help make the world a better place, either through innovations, social reforms or making a contribution to humanitarian causes. Bill Gates has pledged $57 million to help protect young people in Africa against the threat of HIV and Aids.

Sun in Scorpio in Aspect with Neptune

If you were born between 1956 and 1974, whether or not your birthday is listed below, you are likely to feel the influence of Neptune on your Sun.

23 October–1 November in: 1955–62
2–11 November in: 1960–66
12–22 November in: 1965–1970

Bryan Adams	Marie Antoinette	Jill Dando
John Keats	k.d. lang	David Schwimmer

It's not always easy for other people to see the real you behind the image of who they think you are. In fact, it's not always easy for you to know who you are either. You can pick up on other people's fantasies and act out whatever you sense they want you to be. This is a great advantage if you work with the public, because you can instinctively give people what they long for, before they know what that is themselves.

Direct confrontation, even with your own feelings, is rarely easy for you and you may curl yourself up in a tight little ball, refusing to look at situations and hoping that they'll just go away. They rarely do, and giving in to this tendency could be your downfall. Beauty, poetry or the otherworldly could attract you strongly. The poet Keats described himself as being 'half in love with easeful death'. As you empathise easily with human suffering, and long to alleviate it, you can be a natural healer – or you could find death and disability so disturbing that you'll avoid or ignore those who are ill. Some with this combination emit victim signals, like the character Ross, played by David Schwimmer in the sitcom *Friends*, who exudes self-pity and vague disappointment that life isn't going his way. Some –

mercifully only very few – do become real victims, like Jill Dando, who was murdered, and Marie Antoinette, who was guillotined. Most with this aspect, however, will at some time experience a sacrifice of ego power or personal potency. This can transform you, if you'll allow it, as you will then be open to finding an authentic ideal to serve selflessly, which is what you need to be truly fulfilled.

Sun in Scorpio in Aspect with Pluto

If you were born between 1984 and 1995, whether or not your birthday is listed below, you are likely to feel the influence of Pluto on your Sun.

23 October–1 November in: 1939–45 and 1983–88
2–11 November in: 1944–52 and 1987–92
12–22 November in: 1948–57 and 1991–6

| Prince Charles | John Cleese | Marie Curie |
| Charles de Gaulle | The Kray Twins | Lulu |

Pluto, Scorpio's ruler, is the planet of transformation. Its agenda is to serve life by eliminating anything that stands in the way of survival. Your choice is to decide what it is you want to survive – good or evil, the highest values or your own personal interests. The Kray Twins chose the low road and ran a Mafia-style operation in London's East End in the 1960s, running lucrative, and illegal, gambling and drinking clubs, extorting protection money and murdering members of rival gangs. They were eventually sentenced to life imprisonment.

You may choose to get to the root of and eliminate old destructive behaviour patterns, as John Cleese did through group therapy. He wrote about it later with his psychiatrist, Robin Skynner, in *Life and How to Survive It* and *Families and How to Survive Them*, so helping others to heal. You hate hypocrisy and the misuse of power and you're ready to confront anybody, no matter what the cost to yourself. Prince Charles courageously continues to speak out on a number of issues about which he feels passionately, despite an often cruel response from the press.

As you don't find it easy to trust, often because of early experiences of feeling unwanted, you may be rather secretive and self-protective. If you feel betrayed, you may brood, which plays havoc with your sensitive nervous system. Don't forget that the best revenge is to live well. It may take you a long time before you can feel safe enough to show your true self, even to people close to you. It's important that you check your fears against reality. This aspect does tend to heighten paranoia. Life's safer than you think – and you don't have to control everything all the time.

SEVEN

Meeting Your Moon

☾ THE GLYPH FOR THE MOON IS THE SEMI-CIRCLE OR CRESCENT. It is a symbol for the receptiveness of the soul and is associated with feminine energies and the ebb and flow of the rhythms of life. In some traditions it represents the gateway to paradise and the realms of bliss.

The Sun and Moon are the two complementary poles of your personality, like yang and yin, masculine and feminine, active and reflective, career and home, father and mother. The Moon comes into its own as a guide at night, the time of sleeping consciousness. It also has a powerful effect on the waters of the earth. Likewise, the Moon in your birth chart describes what you respond to instinctively and feel 'in your waters', often just below the level of consciousness. It is your private radar system, sending you messages via your body responses and feelings, telling you whether a situation seems safe or scary, nice or nasty. Feelings provide vital information about circumstances in and around you. Ignore them at your peril; that will lead you into emotional, and sometimes even physical, danger. Eating disorders tend to be associated with being out of touch with, or neglecting, the instincts and the body, both of which the Moon describes.

Extraordinary though it might seem to those who are emotionally tuned in, some people have great difficulty in knowing what they are feeling. One simple way is to pay attention to your body. Notice any sensations that attract your attention. Those are linked to your feelings. Now get a sense of whether they are pleasant or unpleasant, then try to put a more exact name to what those feelings might be. Is it sadness, happiness, fear? What is it that they are trying to tell you? Your Moon hints at what will strongly activate your feelings. Learning to trust and decode this information will help make the world seem – and be – a safer place.

The Moon represents your drive to nurture and protect yourself and others. Its sign, house and aspects describe how you respond and adapt emotionally to situations and what feeds you, in every sense of the word. It gives information about your home and home life and how you experienced your mother, family and childhood, as well as describing your comfort zone of what feels familiar – the words 'family' and 'familiar' come from the same source. It shows, too, what makes you feel secure and what could comfort you when you're feeling anxious. Your Moon describes what moves and motivates you powerfully at the deepest instinctual level and indicates what is truly the 'matter' in – or with – your life.

Knowing children's Moon signs can help parents and teachers better understand their insecurities and respect their emotional make-up and needs, and so prevent unnecessary hurt, or even harm, to sensitive young lives. It's all too easy to expect that our children and parents should have the same emotional wiring as we do, but that's rarely how life works. Finding our parents' Moon signs can be a real revelation. It can often help us understand where they are coming from, what they need and why they react to us in the way they do. Many of my clients have been able to find the understanding and compassion to forgive their parents when they realised that they were doing their very best with the emotional resources available to them.

In relationships it is important that your Moon's requirements are met to a good enough extent. For example, if you have your Moon in Sagittarius you must have adventure, freedom and the opportunity to express your beliefs. If being with your partner constantly violates these basic needs, you will never feel secure and loved and the relationship could, in the long term, undermine you. However, if your Moon feels too comfortable, you will never change and grow. The art is to get a good working balance between support and challenge.

A man's Moon sign can show some of the qualities he will unconsciously select in a wife or partner. Some of the others are shown in his Venus sign. Many women can seem much more like their Moon signs than their Sun signs, especially if they are involved in mothering a family and being a support system for their husbands or partners. It is only at the mid-life crisis that many women start to identify more with the qualities of their own Suns rather than living that out through their partners' ambitions. Similarly, men tend to live out the characteristics of their Moon signs through their wives and partners until mid-life, often quite cut off from their own feelings and emotional responses. If a man doesn't seem at all like his Moon sign, then check out the women in his life. There's a good chance that his wife, mother or daughter will show these qualities.

Your Moon can be in any sign, including the same one as your Sun. Each sign belongs to one of the four elements: Fire, Earth, Air or Water. The element of your Moon can give you a general idea of how you respond to new situations and what you need to feel safe and comforted. We all become anxious if our Moon's needs are not being recognised and attended to. We then, automatically, go into our personal little rituals for making ourselves feel better. Whenever you are feeling distressed, especially when you are way out of your comfort zone in an unfamiliar situation, do something to feed and soothe your Moon. You're almost certain to calm down quickly.

Fire Moons

If you have a fire Moon in Aries, Leo or Sagittarius, your first response to any situation is to investigate in your imagination the possibilities for drama, excitement and self-expression. Feeling trapped by dreary routine in an ordinary humdrum life crushes you completely. Knowing that you are carrying out a special mission feeds your soul. To you, all the world's a stage and a voyage of discovery. Unless you are at the centre of the action playing some meaningful role, anxiety and depression can set in. To feel secure, you have to have an appropriate outlet for expressing your spontaneity, honourable instincts and passionate need to be of unique significance. The acknowledgement, appreciation and feedback of people around you are essential, or you don't feel real. Not to be seen and appreciated, or to be overlooked, can feel like a threat to your very existence.

Earth Moons

If you have an earth Moon in Taurus, Virgo or Capricorn, you'll respond to new situations cautiously and practically. Rapidly changing circumstances where you feel swept along and out of control are hard for you to cope with. You need time for impressions to sink in. Sometimes it is only much later, after an event has taken place, that you become sure what you felt about it. Your security lies in slowing down, following familiar routines and rituals, even if they are a bit obsessive, and focusing on something, preferably material – possibly the body itself or nature – which is comforting because it is still there. Indulging the senses in some way often helps too, through food, sex or body care. So does taking charge of the practicalities of the immediate situation, even if this is only mixing the drinks or passing out clipboards. To feel secure, you need continuity and a sense that you have your hand on the rudder of your own life. Think of the rather irreverent joke about the man seeming to cross himself in a crisis, all the while actually touching his most valued possessions to check that they are still intact – spectacles, testicles, wallet and watch. That must have been thought up by someone with the Moon in an earth sign.

Air Moons

When your Moon is in an air sign – Gemini, Libra or Aquarius – you feel most secure when you can stand back from situations and observe them from a distance. Too much intimacy chokes you and you'll tend to escape it by going into your head to the safety of ideas and analysis. Even in close relationships you need your mental, and preferably physical, space. You often have to think, talk or write about what you are feeling before you are sure what your feelings are. By putting them 'out there' so that you can examine them clearly, you can claim them as your own. Unfairness and unethical behaviour can upset you badly and make you feel uneasy until you have done something about it or responded in some way. It can be easy with an air Moon to be unaware of, or to ignore, your own feelings because you are more responsive to ideas, people and situations outside of yourself that may seem to have little connection with you. This is not a good idea, as it cuts you off from the needs of your body as well as your own emotional intelligence. Making opportunities to talk, play with and exchange ideas and information can reduce the stress levels if anxiety strikes.

Water Moons

Finally, if your Moon is in a water sign – Cancer, Scorpio or Pisces – you are ultra-sensitive to atmospheres, and you can experience other people's pain or distress as if they were your own. You tend to take everything personally and, even if the situation has nothing at all to do with you, feel responsible for making it better. Your worst nightmare is to feel no emotional response coming back from other people. That activates your deep-seated terror of abandonment, which can make you feel that you don't exist and is, quite literally, what you fear even more than death. If you feel insecure, you may be tempted to resort to emotional manipulation to try to force intimacy with others – not a good idea, as this can lead to the very rejection that you dread. You are at your most secure when the emotional climate is positive and you have trusted, supportive folk around who will winkle you out of hiding if you become too reclusive. With a water Moon, it is vital to learn to value your own feelings and to take them seriously – and to have a safe, private place you can retreat to when you feel emotionally fragile. As you never forget anything which has made a feeling impression on you, sometimes your reactions are triggered by unconscious memories of things long past, rather than what is taking place in the present. When you learn to interpret them correctly, your feelings are your finest ally and will serve you well.

Finding Your Moon Sign

If you don't yet know your Moon sign, before looking it up, you could have some fun reading through the descriptions that follow and seeing if you can guess which one it is. To find your Moon sign, check your year and date of birth in the tables on pp. 100–113. For a greater in-depth understanding of your Moon sign, you might like to read about its characteristics in the book in this series about that sign.

At the beginning of each section are the names of some well-known Scorpios with that particular Moon sign. You can find more about them in Chapter Ten.

Sun in Scorpio with Moon in Aries

Benvenuto Cellini	John Cleese	Linda Evans
Bill Gates	Martin Luther	Meg Ryan

Security and comfort for you means being in charge. Your task is to develop the courage to stand up for yourself and have your own needs met, without bullying or being bullied. When roused, you'll boldly go where no man – or woman – has ever gone before. Bill Gates didn't become a computer billionaire by hanging back, waiting to see what everyone else would do first. Your tendency is to act spontaneously and then deal with the consequences later. This can go along with a temper that's incandescent – like John Cleese's explosive character Basil, in *Fawlty Towers*. Fortunately, most can control their passions better than the short-fused sixteenth-century goldsmith and sculptor Benvenuto Cellini. By his own admission, he had no hesitation in maiming or even murdering people who thwarted him. If you want something, you tend to go for it and you can be breathtakingly self-willed. This hot-headed impulsiveness could land you in trouble time and again.

Action and drama are food for your soul. Aries at its best is undiluted heroism and there's nothing that stirs your blood so much as a hefty challenge to sink your teeth into, often the bigger and tougher the better. Challenges don't come much bigger or tougher than confronting, single-handed, the political might of the medieval church – in today's terms, it's bit like taking on every multi-national company on the planet at once. That's what Martin Luther did because he was so outraged by the blatant corruption of the church authorities. What's more, he won. Your greatest victory comes when you understand and master yourself – especially your anger, or apparent lack of it – and then go on to make a significant mark on the outside world.

Sun in Scorpio with Moon in Taurus

Prince Charles	Peter Cook	Richard Dreyfuss
The Walton sextuplets	Demi Moore	Erwin Rommel

Having your Sun and Moon in fixed signs gives you determination and resolve. Once you've set your sights on a target, you'll rarely deviate from your course until you've achieved it. With so much time and energy invested, it's important to check occasionally whether adjustments are needed along the way. This isn't always easy. As you wouldn't stick to your guns if you didn't believe you were right, you may not see the point of self-questioning, but a little objectivity can save you from running up against a brick wall. Your practical and common-sense approach to whatever life throws at you makes you a dependable rock for everyone around. Like a still pool of peace, your presence is calming and reassuring.

Security for you lies in life's basics – owning your own home, enough money in the bank and food in the fridge, plus regular, satisfying sex – as well as a sense of being in control. You don't like it when events move too fast. It's not that you can't handle change, you just need time, sometimes a very long time, to assimilate new situations and to adjust. Material security is of the utmost importance to you. If your bank balance sinks below a certain level, your anxiety will rise. The German commander Rommel was sentenced to death for supporting a plot to kill Hitler. He was given the choice of firing squad or suicide and chose suicide – because it preserved his estate for his family. Recharging your batteries is often best done by getting back in tune with the slow rhythm of the seasons. An hour or two in the garden, composting or hacking back the deadwood, can restore your composure beautifully.

Sun in Scorpio with Moon in Gemini

Tina Brown   Margaret Mitchell   Nicholas Culpeper
Fyodor Dostoevsky   Goldie Hawn   Auguste Rodin

Incurably curious, and sometimes downright nosy, you delight in keeping up-to-date with whatever is current in your field and have an uncanny ability – and often the ruthlessness – to separate dead ducks from dead certainties, speedily. An adolescent at heart, you're a free spirit and hate to be tied down. Running on so much nervous energy, it could be easy for you to lose focus and fritter away your stamina. Being able to communicate is as essential to you as breathing, and keeping a journal or finding a place to air your troubles can be vital tools in your emotional first-aid kit. Any knowledge you have, you like to pass on. Nicholas

Culpeper translated the *London Dispensatory* [*sic*] from Latin into English, making it available to everyone and so breaking the medical monopoly. It made him powerful enemies, but he didn't care, as the barbed comments sprinkled liberally throughout his more famous *Complete Herbal* show.

With your needle-sharp responses, sexual innuendoes and occasional poisoned verbal darts, you're hard to outdo when it comes to mental gymnastics. Lightning-quick analysis and lateral thinking are your great strengths. You can use your clever tongue to keep control of situations and you do love to have the last word. You can also be a thorough charmer and incorrigible flirt and could sell snowballs to Siberia. With your low boredom threshold, a career which offers plenty of variety, the chance to get out and about and meet and communicate with new people, combined with the opportunity to work with life's deep, dark or dangerous side, would suit you perfectly. Medicine, psychology, selling funerals or life insurance, revamping just about anything, or investigative journalism could all be right up your street.

Sun in Scorpio with Moon in Cancer

Tatum O'Neal   Boris Becker   Sir George Trevelyan
David and Frederick   Condoleeza Rice   Bo Derek
Barclay

Being highly intuitive, emotional atmospheres impact on you instantly. While what you feel is always valid, how you interpret this could be wide of the mark – because you also pick up on other people's feelings and experience them as if they were your own. You have, too, acutely sensitive antennae – set permanently at high on threat alert – and an exceptionally retentive memory bank for all that you've ever experienced emotionally. Your challenge is to identify what you are responding to in the here and now, as opposed to being caught up in re-runs of ancient dramas – and to separate out your own feelings from those of people around you. By doing so, you'll free yourself from ancient emotional baggage as well as unnecessary angst, and allow your capacity for tenderness to blossom safely.

Those to whom you feel connected are at the centre of your world and you rely on them heavily for support and protection. The very thought of their loss or withdrawal devastates you. You feel deeply and are easily moved to tears, something you may try to suppress ruthlessly, especially if you're a man. You've strong reclusive tendencies. The publicity-shy newspaper magnates, the Barclay twins, have built themselves a virtual fortress on the Channel Island of Sark. You could use your extensive emotional armoury to try to control everyone and everything around you. As that usually backfires and leaves you isolated, it's best to recognise that you are strong enough in your vulnerability to deal courageously with anything that comes your way. Finding ways of discharging strong feelings, especially resentment, is essential for your well-being – as is surrounding yourself with those you love, and who, in turn, adore you.

Sun in Scorpio with Moon in Leo

Lauren Hutton	Joseph McCarthy	President Nehru
William Penn	Julia Roberts	Leon Trotsky

Your instinct in any situation is to gravitate to the seat of power and occupy a central position. This may not always be obvious to watchers, as you tend to keep your motives, and methods, well hidden. More than likely, you're a born leader, with formidable organising skills. If you were ignored and put down as a child, and weren't allowed to be spontaneous, you may be hungry for attention and try to hog the limelight, elbowing others out of the way. Your Leo Moon needs a role to play and plenty of admiring attention to keep you feeling secure. Your challenge is to make sure that the role you choose brings out the best, and not the worst, of this combination.

Fortunately, few are as twisted as US Senator Joseph McCarthy, later described as a 'pathological character assassin'. He rose suddenly from near-obscurity in 1950 to appoint himself chief inquisitor in a witch-hunt against – usually imaginary – communists, often in the full glare of television cameras, and in the process destroyed many lives.

Playing an honourable role, that allows you to stand in the spotlight radiating generosity and integrity, and possibly exposing genuine corruption, suits you much better. Despite your shyness, part of you adores being a glamorous party animal. You probably love getting dressed up beautifully and being made a fuss of, too. When every eye is turned your way and you're looking your best, then all's well in your world. Ambition and self-promotion come easily to you. You expect the finest and usually get it. Learning to unwind and play with children can be a great tonic, as they can help bring out the spontaneous child in you.

Sun in Scorpio with Moon in Virgo

Fenella Fielding	Jodie Foster	k.d. lang
Viscount Linley	Gordon Ramsay	Sir Jimmy Savile

You take pride in doing things well, and producing finely crafted work gives you a quiet sense of happiness and satisfaction. Finding tasks that you see as being useful, of service, or leading to some clearly defined end-result helps keep you grounded. In any creative field you make a skilled artist and craftsperson, going to endless trouble to get the finished article just right. Viscount Linley, Princess Margaret's son, is a highly creative furniture-maker, specialising in meticulously detailed marquetry work.

You may need to guard against a tendency to be fiercely critical, both of yourself and others, when things don't come up to your sometimes impossibly high standards. While you'll enjoy ticking off achievements on those never-ending to-do lists that whirr round in your head, it's best not to let them run your life. You're not afraid of hard work – in fact, you thrive on it – but take care not to become a workaholic. With your solid common sense, organisation skills and sharp eye for flaws, you can be a gifted problem-solver. One of Sir Jimmy Savile's best-loved shows was *Jim'll Fix It*. You may have an interest in body care or be drawn to the healing professions, where you could excel. When you feel insecure, you may work even harder and end up frazzled. Your nervous system is highly strung, so quiet time alone for rest, recuperation and reflection is essential. Orderly rituals, even simple ones like laying out the tools of your trade or clipping your nails carefully, can be immensely comforting in times of stress. Simplicity suits you, so cutting down to essentials, dejunking your life and detoxing your body could be a perfect tonic from time to time.

Sun in Scorpio with Moon in Libra

Marie Antoinette	Leonardo Di Caprio	Alistair Cooke
Billie Jean King	Sylvia Plath	Ted Turner

Scorpio's desire for power and Libra's passion for peace and justice, as well as a talent for strategy, make you a front-line candidate for politics. Alistair Cooke's broadcast of *Letter from America*, which ran for over half a century, aimed at giving a relatively balanced view of American politics. Billie Jean King, after a highly successful career as a top tennis player, played a prominent role in campaigning for better pay and conditions for women in the sport. Alternatively – or additionally – the Scorpionic sex drive and Libran love of romance can pull you towards multiple romantic dalliances. Broadcasting tycoon Ted Turner, one-time husband of Jane Fonda and notorious ladies' man, also gifted $1 billion to a new foundation to support the United Nations.

At times you are idealistic to the point of naivety and may have unrealistic expectations of relationships, or life itself. If there's disharmony around, or you sense someone's offended, you'll feel edgy until it's sorted out. With your keen sense of justice, you can see everybody's viewpoint, yet sometimes forget your own. If you feel you've been wronged, though, you can brood and fret about being treated unfairly. Your natural elegance and relaxed manner make people feel at ease, but behind that gentleness and courtesy is the mind of a general. You can size up opponents shrewdly, assess where they're coming from, then bide your time and pounce at just the right moment. It's easy to get your own way with the minimum of effort. You simply convince others that it was their idea in the first place. With your appreciation of elegance and luxury, you do like the finer things in life and a home full of artwork, flowers and light could bring you great comfort.

Sun in Scorpio with Moon in Scorpio

Björk	Adolf Driesch	Althea Flynt
Whoopi Goldberg	The Grand Duchess Olga	David Schwimmer

As a child, you would have been aware of the undercurrents of power or topics that were taboo in your family or community. You may even have witnessed the more brutal or bruising side of life, which could have left you with the belief that the world is a dangerous, or even evil, place and nobody is to be trusted. The father of Althea Flynt, publisher of the porn magazine *Hustler*, went on the rampage when she was eight, killing his wife, himself and two others. She turned to heroin after her husband's spine was shattered by a gunman and died in her bath of an AIDS-related illness. That's extreme, but life is unlikely to allow you to remain naive.

You tend to be secretive about your true feelings, revealing them only when you are absolutely sure you can trust your confidant, or never at all. You could be pre-occupied with sex, power, death and the occult, and these themes may thread their way through your life and career. This is an excellent mix for researching any of these areas, as did Adolf Driesch, a philosophy professor who both founded experimental embryology and investigated parapsychology. On a slightly lighter note, Whoopi Goldberg at one time worked as a beautician for an undertaker.

You probably radiate charisma and smouldering sexuality and make a rock-solid friend but a fearsome enemy. It is important to discharge your emotional sewage tanks regularly. Sex can help, and so can confronting your fears through therapy. Your greatest challenge is to refuse to be a victim and to use your formidable willpower, insight and honesty to drop the ghosts of the past and create a better and more authentic future for everyone, yourself included.

Sun in Scorpio with Moon in Sagittarius

| Billy Graham | Rock Hudson | Mahalia Jackson |
| Cleo Laine | Lulu | Pablo Picasso |

You're almost certainly a natural philosopher, whether this comes out as a full-blown search for the meaning of life or simply an ability to shrug off with a smile the inevitable dark days and disappointments that are part of life's package. Sunny Sagittarius gives you faith in life – and you love to pass on this optimism, together with whatever else you've learned, or believe, about the human condition. Your whole-hearted approach and passionate delivery can be infectious, inspiring others to better things. Charismatic and crusading evangelist Billy Graham has travelled the world over speaking to packed stadiums, and through television, films and books has inspired millions to convert to Christianity. Despite many of his kind being caught with their fingers in the till or trousers down, investigations have consistently found Graham to be a man of the highest moral stature and integrity. Faith, and the hope of salvation, was the message, too, of Mahalia Jackson, considered by many to be the greatest gospel singer ever.

You've a constant itch to move on that can be physical, mental or restlessly romantic, with a deep-seated need to explore new faces, places and ideas. The painter Picasso believed that the meaning of life could be found in art, and loved playing with different styles, as in his 'blue period' and 'rose period'. His love life was correspondingly experimental. You can see the possibilities in every situation and may even be a bit of an opportunist. You need a partner who can share your enthusiasms and will give you plenty of freedom, as you love adventure and hate confinement. You make a wonderful promoter, publisher or entrepreneur, trusting your hunches and happy to chance your luck, which usually pays off, provided you don't push it too far.

Sun in Scorpio with Moon in Capricorn

| Bryan Adams | George Eliot | Indira Gandhi |
| Barbara Hutton | The Kray Twins | Jean Rook |

A Capricorn Moon can often mean deprivation or heavy responsibilities in childhood, either because your background was poor or humble, or your parents were elderly, strict or ill. It could also be that, even though material circumstances were comfortable or even luxurious, correct behaviour and discipline were the rule, rather than spontaneity and warm acceptance. Barbara Hutton, one of the wealthiest heiresses in the world, was called the 'poor little rich girl' after her mother committed suicide when she was four, and she went on to have seven unsuccessful marriages and battle with drink, drugs and anorexia.

For many, though, early hardships are an excellent

training for life and stiffen the moral fibre. With your capacity for hard work, self-discipline and instinct for long-term planning, there is almost nothing you can't achieve if you put your mind to it. The brassy and abrasive tabloid journalist Jean Rook only missed a deadline twice in 20 years, once on the birth of her son, the other when she was diagnosed with cancer. Once you've set your sights on a goal, you will stick at it doggedly, overcoming every obstacle until success is yours. You are well able to look after yourself and unless you give in to the periodic depression that can dog you, you're headed straight up the ladder of success. What Barbara Hutton may have lacked was the long-term goals and ambitions – and tough obstacles to overcome – that make this combination feel secure. Status, power and respect are what you crave, in whatever hierarchy of power you find yourself, whether it is the political arena, like Indira Gandhi, or the gangland pecking order of London's East End, like the Kray twins. As solitude and melancholy feed you, it's important to allow yourself plenty of time alone, as well as getting off the work treadmill occasionally to enjoy the fruits of your considerable labours.

Sun in Scorpio with Moon in Aquarius

Albert Camus   George Gallup   Alexandra David-Néel
Calista Flockhart Captain James Cook   Vivien Leigh

The French writer Albert Camus had an international success with *The Outsider*, a book whose main character is alienated from society because he is different and doesn't care about social rules and conventions. To make matters worse, he refuses to lie in order to fit in and make his life easier. These themes – feeling like an alien or outsider and being ruthlessly honest about how you see the world – are ones that are familiar to those with this combination.

Your Aquarius Moon is tuned in to the need for change in society at large. George Gallup was the founder of the first public opinion polls that allowed the ideas of ordinary people to be known and taken into account. You can feel injustice and lack of humanity acutely, but it's less easy for you to be aware of your own feelings, personal needs or those of your body. You may even forget to eat or sleep regularly.

Your home or family background is likely to be unusual or nonconformist in some way and, even if you have lived in the same place all your life, you could feel slightly unsettled, as if you are just camping, waiting to move on. Being associated with groups of like-minded people may be a great comfort to you. You hate elitism and restraints and, in relationships, need plenty of freedom. Even if you don't see your friends or family for years on end, and they live scattered across the world, you can still feel strongly bonded to them. Alexandra David-Néel went off travelling for 18 months but it was 14 years before her husband saw her again. Seeing the world as your family can make you feel more secure and at home on planet Earth.

Sun in Scorpio with Moon in Pisces

Marie Curie	Martin Scorsese	Joni Mitchell
Winona Ryder	Princess Grace of Monaco	Robert Louis Stevenson

You are often better at sticking up for others, especially those that life has wounded, than you are for yourself. You can read emotional atmospheres and empathise instinctively with the pain of others, and so become a magnet for victims looking for the help you are so free in giving, and long for so much yourself. Don't let your caring and self-sacrifice go too far, or you could end up ensnared in the compassion trap. The more unscrupulous can use this near-psychic combination to manipulate the unwary. Others can spot a con instantly, and retaliate.

Pisces is the sign of retreat, dreams, illusion, spirituality and sacrifice, and your childhood and career are likely to be threaded through with some of these themes. Winona Ryder's parents lived the hippy dream; drug guru Timothy Leary was her godfather. Both Robert Louis Stevenson and Martin Scorsese were sickly when young; this tends to develop the imagination, as so much time is spent alone and cut off from the world. Scorsese trained as a priest for a year before going to film school and Stevenson's best-loved work, *Treasure Island*, was inspired by a tiny pond with an island seen from his window during childhood illnesses.

Public figures with Pisces Moons can pick up instantly, and provide, the fantasy their audience longs for, just as Grace Kelly became the fairy-tale Princess Grace of Monaco, a far cry from the life of sex and secrets she actually led. Frequent retreats from everyday reality, which can often feel like a vale of tears, are essential for your well-being. It's best if that escape does not come through alcohol or food, as this can get out of hand. Meditation, art, music or even just daydreaming are much healthier options.

EIGHT

Mercury – It's All in the Mind

THE GLYPHS FOR THE PLANETS ARE MADE UP OF THREE SYMBOLS: the circle, the semi-circle and the cross. Mercury is the only planet, apart from Pluto, whose glyph is made up of all three of these symbols. At the bottom there is the cross, representing the material world; at the top is the semi-circle of the crescent Moon, symbolising the personal soul; and in the middle, linking these two, is the circle of eternity, expressed through the individual. In mythology, Mercury was the only god who had access to all three worlds – the underworld, the middle world of earth and the higher world of the gods. Mercury in your chart represents your ability, through your thoughts and words, to make connections between the inner world of your mind and emotions, the outer world of other people and events, and the higher world of intuition. Your Mercury sign can give you a great deal of information about the way your mind works and about your interests, communication skills and your preferred learning style.

It can be frustrating when we just can't get through to some people and it's easy to dismiss them as being either completely thick or deliberately obstructive. Chances are they are neither. It may be that you're simply not talking each other's languages. Knowing your own and other people's communication styles can lead to major breakthroughs in relationships.

Information about children's natural learning patterns can help us teach them more effectively. It's impossible to learn properly if the material isn't presented in a way that resonates with the way your mind works. You just can't 'hear' it, pick it up or grasp it. Wires then get crossed and the data simply isn't processed. Many children are seriously disadvantaged if learning materials and environments don't speak to them. You may even have been a child like that yourself. If so, you could easily have been left with the false impression that you are a poor learner just because you couldn't get a handle on the lessons being taught. Identifying your own learning style can be like finding the hidden key to the treasure room of knowledge.

The signs of the zodiac are divided into four groups by element:

> The fire signs: Aries, Leo and Sagittarius
> The earth signs: Taurus, Virgo and Capricorn
> The air signs: Gemini, Libra and Aquarius
> The water signs: Cancer, Scorpio and Pisces

Your Mercury will therefore belong to one of the four elements, depending on which sign it is in. Your Mercury can only be in one of three signs – the same sign as your Sun, the one before or the one after. This means that each sign has one learning style that is never natural to it. For Scorpio, this is the earth style.

Mercury in each of the elements has a distinctive way of

operating. I've given the following names to the learning and communicating styles of Mercury through the elements. Mercury in fire – active imaginative; Mercury in earth – practical; Mercury in air – logical; and Mercury in water – impressionable.

Mercury in Fire: Active Imaginative

Your mind is wide open to the excitement of fresh ideas. It responds to action and to the creative possibilities of new situations. Drama, games and storytelling are excellent ways for you to learn. You love to have fun and play with ideas. Any material to be learned has to have some significance for you personally, or add to your self-esteem, otherwise you rapidly lose interest. You learn by acting out the new information, either physically or in your imagination. The most efficient way of succeeding in any goal is to make first a mental picture of your having achieved it. This is called mental rehearsal and is used by many top sportsmen and women as a technique to help improve their performance. You do this spontaneously, as your imagination is your greatest mental asset. You can run through future scenarios in your mind's eye and see, instantly, where a particular piece of information or situation could lead and spot possibilities that other people couldn't even begin to dream of. You are brilliant at coming up with flashes of inspiration for creative breakthroughs and crisis management.

Mercury in Earth: Practical

Endless presentations of feelings, theories and possibilities can make your eyes glaze over and your brain ache to shut down. What really turns you on is trying out these theories and possibilities to see if they work in practice. If they don't, you'll tend to classify them 'of no further interest'. Emotionally charged information is at best a puzzling non-starter and at worst an irritating turn-off. Practical demonstrations, tried and tested facts and working models fascinate you. Hands-on learning, where you can see how a process functions from start to finish, especially if it leads to some useful material end-product, is right up your street. It's important to allow yourself plenty of time when you are learning, writing or thinking out what to say, otherwise you can feel rushed and out of control, never pleasant sensations for earth signs. Your special skill is in coming up with effective solutions to practical problems and in formulating long-range plans that bring concrete, measurable results.

Mercury in Air: Logical

You love learning about, and playing with, ideas, theories and principles. Often you do this best by arguing or bouncing ideas off other people, or by writing down your thoughts. Your special gift is in your ability to stand back and work out the patterns of relationship between people or things. You much prefer it when facts are presented to you logically and unemotionally and have very little time for the irrational, uncertainty or for personal opinions. You do, though, tend to have plenty of those kinds of views yourself, only you call them logical conclusions. Whether a fact is useful or not is less important than whether it fits into your mental map of how the world operates. If facts don't fit in, you'll either ignore them, find a way of making them fit, or, occasionally, make a grand leap to a new, upgraded theory. Yours is the mind of the scientist or chess player. You make a brilliant planner because you can be detached enough to take an overview of the entire situation.

Mercury in Water: Impressionable

Your mind is sensitive to atmospheres and emotional undertones and to the context in which information is presented. Plain facts and figures can often leave you cold and even intimidated. You can take things too personally and read between the lines for what you believe is really being said or taught. If you don't feel emotionally safe, you can be cautious about revealing your true thoughts. It may be hard, or even impossible, for you to learn properly in what you sense is a hostile environment. You are excellent at impression management. Like a skilful artist painting a picture, you can influence others to think what you'd like them to by using suggestive gestures or pauses and intonations. People with Mercury in water signs are often seriously disadvantaged by left-brain schooling methods that are too rigidly structured for them. You take in information best through pictures or images, so that you get a 'feel' for the material and can make an emotional bond with it, in the same way you connect with people. In emotionally supportive situations where there is a rapport between you and your instructors, or your learning material, you are able just to drink in and absorb circulating knowledge without conscious effort, sometimes not even being clear about how or why you know certain things.

Finding Your Mercury Sign

If you don't yet know your Mercury sign, you might like to see if you can guess what it is from the descriptions below before checking it out in the tables on pp.114–15.

Sun in Scorpio with Mercury in Libra

Jill Dando	Leonardo Di Caprio	Bill Gates
Napoleon Hill	k.d. lang	Robin Day

This can be a formidable combination for succeeding at whatever you put your mind to, linking as it does your Scorpionic desire for control with the mind-set of a general. Your ability to consider everyone's point of view, and deliberate on any future moves they might make, allows you to run rings round the less clear-thinking and win any battle before it has even begun. Napoleon Hill spent twenty years researching the laws of success and his *Think and Grow Rich*, published in 1937, is still one of the best books of its kind.

You could be an excellent negotiator and diplomat and rarely need to resort to direct confrontation – unless you choose to. Through courtesy and tactical persuasion, you can easily convince others that you are on their side, even when you're not and have plans of your own up your sleeve. You are an accomplished debater; in fact, you learn best by putting out an idea or an opinion, and seeing how it's received. Often you don't know what you think until you've aired a variety of positions and finally come to the one that seems to be the most balanced. You can find just the right words to be a skilful peacemaker, but are also capable of playing devil's advocate and taking up an opposing side if you think it is being under-represented, and sometimes just for the hell of it. Principles and justice matter to you and you are unlikely to desert them, even if you are backed into a corner. You much prefer making fair deals where all parties make equal contributions or concessions and everyone is happy with the final outcome.

Sun in Scorpio with Mercury in Scorpio

Prince Charles	Hillary Clinton	Terry Gilliam
Princess Grace	Billy Graham	The Kray Twins
of Monaco		

No matter how friendly you appear, you'll usually prefer to keep your thoughts private and to guard your privacy, quietly but firmly. You may or may not have anything to hide, but that's nobody's business but your own. Hillary Clinton maintained a dignified silence as the world's press revealed humiliating details of her husband's sexual adventures. Your thoughts may be deep, dark and dangerous, and you could obsess over resentments, plotting revenge and retribution, and end up being consumed by your own bitterness. It's usually better to get what's bothering you off your chest and air it or act on it. The work of cartoonist Terry Gilliam, of the *Monty Python* team, takes the sting out of Scorpionic fantasies of sex and violence by making them so grotesque that they become hilarious.

Money, sex and the struggle for survival are rarely far from your thoughts, which ensures that these things do come into your life – one way or another. Many with no belief in an afterlife are terrified of death. Others, who fear divine retribution, may try to make deals with the Almighty as an insurance against future trouble, while some make genuine attempts to transform their lives. You could be a first-class sleuth or researcher, as, once you become interested in a subject, nothing about it is likely to escape your notice. Your speciality is noticing cover-ups, scams and hypocrisy, which you'll feel compelled to deal with, even though you may be shaking in your shoes. Being so intuitive, you'll probably prefer to communicate in person or by phone, as then you can pick up clues about what a person is really feeling, allowing you to respond more appropriately to the situation.

Sun in Scorpio with Mercury in Sagittarius

Marie Curie	George Eliot	Edmond Halley
Goldie Hawn	Martin Luther	Erwin Rommel

No matter how dark life seems, your thoughts can slice through the gloom to reveal rainbows and silver linings. Your vision is broad and your mind wide open to fresh experiences and to learning from people of every race, creed and culture. Victorian writer George Eliot, author of *Middlemarch*, laid the foundations for the modern novel by exploring moral problems and analysing the psychology of her characters. It is said that her gift is in allowing readers to appreciate the lives of people who are quite different from themselves.

Mercury in Sagittarius gives generosity of mind and spirit, a talent for inspiring and encouraging others, and a knack of being lucky with your hunches. Edmond Halley, who had a comet named after him because he correctly predicted the date of its return, encouraged Isaac Newton to publish his ground-breaking book on his theories of gravity – then edited it and paid for its publication out of his own pocket. You have little fear of taking on big projects because of your optimism and faith that it will all work out somehow, but you may need to make sure that you don't promise, in the heat of the moment, more than you can deliver when your enthusiasm has died down. Travelling, advising, publishing, widening your mental horizons, morality or the meaning of life could fascinate you. Your tendency to be outspoken and sometimes tactless can land you in hot water. Martin Luther left no one in any doubt as to his beliefs when he nailed his lengthy protest at corrupt religious practices to a church door in 1517, and so started the Reformation. It is said that he possessed the power of kindling others with the fire of his own convictions. You do, too.

NINE

Venus – At Your Pleasure

♀ THE GLYPH FOR VENUS IS MADE UP OF THE CIRCLE OF ETERNITY on top of the cross of matter. Esoterically this represents love, which is a quality of the divine, revealed on earth through personal choice. The saying 'One man's meat is another man's poison' couldn't be more relevant when it comes to what we love. It is a mystery why we find one thing attractive and another unattractive, or even repulsive. Looking at the sign, aspects and house of your Venus can't give any explanation of this mystery, but it can give some clear indications of what it is that you value and find desirable. This can be quite different from what current fashion tells you you should like. For example, many people are strongly turned on by voluptuous bodies but the media constantly shows images of near-anorexics as the desirable ideal. If you ignore what you, personally, find beautiful and try to be, or to love, what at heart leaves you cold, you are setting yourself up for unnecessary pain and dissatisfaction. Being true to your Venus sign, even if other people think you are strange, brings joy and pleasure. It also builds up your self-esteem because it grounds you solidly in your own personal values. This, in turn, makes you much more attractive to others. Not only that, it improves your relationships immeasurably, because you are living authentically and not betraying yourself by trying to prove your worth to others by being something you are not.

Glittering Venus, the brightest planet in the heavens, was named after the goddess of love, war and victory. Earlier names for her were Aphrodite, Innana and Ishtar. She was beautiful, self-willed and self-indulgent but was also skilled in all the arts of civilisation.

Your Venus sign shows what you desire and would like to possess, not only in relationships but also in all aspects of your taste, from clothes and culture to hobbies and hobby-horses. It identifies how and where you can be charming and seductive and skilful at creating your own type of beauty yourself. It also describes your style of attracting partners and the kind of people that turn you on. When your Venus is activated you feel powerful, desirable and wonderfully, wickedly indulged and indulgent. When it is not, even if someone has all the right credentials to make a good match, the relationship will always lack that certain something. If you don't take the chance to express your Venus to a good enough degree somewhere in your life, you miss out woefully on delight and happiness.

Morning Star, Evening Star

Venus appears in the sky either in the morning or in the evening. The ancients launched their attacks when Venus became a morning star, believing that she was then in her warrior-goddess role, releasing aggressive energy for victory in battle. If you're a morning-star person, you're likely to be impulsive, self-willed and idealistic, prepared to hold out until you find the partner who is just right for you.

Relationships and business dealings of morning-star Venus people are said to prosper best whenever Venus in the sky is a morning star. If you are an early bird, you can check this out. At these times Venus can be seen in the eastern sky before the Sun has risen.

The name for Venus as an evening star is Hesperus and it was then, traditionally, said to be sacred to lovers. Evening-star people tend to be easy-going and are open to negotiation, conciliation and making peace. If you are an evening-star Venus person, your best times in relationship and business affairs are said to be when Venus can be seen, jewel-like, in the western sky after the Sun has set.

Because the orbit of Venus is so close to the Sun, your Venus can only be in one of five signs. You have a morning-star Venus if your Venus is in one of the two signs that come before your Sun sign in the zodiac. You have an evening-star Venus if your Venus is in either of the two signs that follow your Sun sign. If you have Venus in the same sign as your Sun, you could be either, depending on whether your Venus is ahead of or behind your Sun. (You can find out which at the author's website www.janeridderpatrick.com.)

If you don't yet know your Venus sign, you might like to read through all of the following descriptions and see if you can guess what it is. You can find out for sure on pp.116–18.

At the beginning of each section are the names of some well-known Scorpios with that particular Venus sign. You can find out more about them in Chapter Ten, Famous Scorpio Birthdays.

Sun in Scorpio with Venus in Virgo

Sarah Bernhardt	Nigel Havers	Joni Mitchell
Sylvia Plath	Julia Roberts	Evelyn Waugh

Little gives you as much pleasure as a job well done and you'll take delight in honing your skills as life goes on. You may have to be careful not to become a workaholic or too fussy and critical, as this could rob you of joy and damage your relationships. You need a partner whose mind and professionalism you can admire and respect, especially for their wit, refined tastes and skills. You may enjoy running your home – or your mind or body – in an efficient and orderly fashion and have an interest in health and hygiene. You may even be fascinated by rituals and taking things apart to find out how they work. Writers, actors and artists with this combination take great pride in getting the details right and constantly upgrading their expertise and perfecting their craft.

Nothing will enhance your self-esteem more than identifying and sticking to your guns about doing what you believe is appropriate in every situation, no matter what others might think or how they react. You may choose, like the ancient virgin goddesses, to give yourself sexually as you please, with or without the obligations of marriage. Sarah Bernhardt, reckoned to be the most versatile actress of all time, had a stream of lovers from princes to penniless authors and only, briefly, married once. Even if you do marry or commit there is part of you that belongs to you alone. Selling out on this for the sake of a relationship compromises your integrity and only leads to grief. Your challenge is to find a place in your life for both passionate involvement and cool self-possession.

Sun in Scorpio with Venus in Libra

| Boris Becker | Prince Charles | Jill Dando |
| Bo Derek | Princess Grace of Monaco | Pablo Picasso |

Elegance and grace thrill you, and you like your partners to be both intelligent and easy on the eye. You're a stylish lover, and enjoy the full works in romance – flowers, candlelit dinners and teasing flirtation. A partnership of some kind is vital for your happiness – and so is plenty of satisfying sex. If your heart is untouched, you'd prefer your dalliances to be civilised understandings, with the minimum of fuss and no hard feelings when it's time to move on. Checking that you and your partner are agreeing to the same contract, though, can save endless trouble. Despite the passion of your Scorpio Sun, love itself may remain a bit of an abstract idea. When asked, on his engagement, whether he was in love, Prince Charles replied that he was, rather spoiling the effect by adding 'whatever love means'. But when you do experience the impact of true love, you'll feel bereft if your partner's not constantly by your side.

Little upsets you more than injustice and disharmony and you'll go to great lengths to put the balance right, even if you have to ruffle a few feathers in the process. Prince Charles is obviously deeply pained by the lack of harmony and proportion in some modern architecture and has spoken out publicly, calling one building 'a monstrous carbuncle'. He is himself a gifted watercolour painter. You like to be liked but you need to be careful not to be swayed from your own good judgement and give way to other people too much just to be seen as Ms or Mr Nice. Many with this combination keep their private passions under wraps, and present only their charm and best profile to the world.

Sun in Scorpio with Venus in Scorpio

Benjamin Britten	Hillary Clinton	Jodie Foster
Charles Manson	Demi Moore	Meg Ryan

Sex and power, as well as the mysteries of life and death, fascinate you, and it's here you'll find your happiness, even if you break taboos. Think of Meg Ryan's character having fun faking an orgasm in a busy restaurant in *When Harry Met Sally*. Demi Moore hired three cameramen to film the birth of her first child. Few, fortunately, have their ideas of pleasure so twisted by the need for power as psychopath Charles Manson, who was jailed for life for brutal, ritualistic murders, including that of the actress Sharon Tate, who was eight months pregnant. The true joy in this combination comes when you have the courage to look the hidden and the forbidden fully in the face and stake your claim on what you love. The composer Benjamin Britten was gay at a time when active homosexuality could result in a prison sentence. Despite this, he found an illicit love that lasted until death parted them after nearly 40 years – and explicitly instructed his biographer to tell the truth about him and his lover.

Beneath your seemingly calm exterior beats a passionate and often possessive heart. You are intensely private and may be secretive about what is really going on in your life. There can be much agony and ecstasy behind closed doors – and love triangles could feature. If this happens, it can be a gateway to greater strength, forcing you to choose, and act on, what you value most highly. Occasionally, this combination may indicate abusive, manipulative or degrading experiences of 'love'. If this has been your experience, know that it doesn't have to stay that way. You have almost unlimited power to transform your relationships, especially the one with yourself. Bullies – and those include your own fears – are cowards. By standing up to them, your strength and self-esteem will grow.

Sun in Scorpio with Venus in Sagittarius

Charles Atlas	Christiaan Barnard	George Eliot
Whoopi Goldberg	Sir Oswald Mosley	Robert Louis Stevenson

Sagittarius is the sign of teaching, preaching, showmanship, adventure, gambling and travel and, in one form or another, those are the areas where you'll find your bliss. Despite your shy exterior, you can be gifted at publicity and promotion, either for yourself or others, and this could give you quite a buzz. Charles Atlas was famous for his advertising campaign for his body-building course. It first showed a seven-stone weakling having sand kicked in his face by a beach pest, then, after following the Charles Atlas course, the same man, with bulging muscles, punching the bully in front of his impressed girlfriend. That advertisement captures beautifully Sagittarian salesmanship combined with Scorpio's love of revenge.

Whatever your gospel – and you're almost certain to have one – you'll take enormous pleasure in tub-thumping it with fiery zeal and conviction. You have opinions and no way are you going to keep them to yourself, even if you are locked up because of them, as was Oswald Mosley, the aristocratic fascist leader during the Second World War. You may find yourself in the role of teacher or student with someone you love. Foreigners could also intrigue you. Like Robert Louis Stevenson, you could marry one and go travelling together – and prefer travelling to arriving. You or your partner may be connected with sport, publishing or the legal profession. Being a free spirit, you hate to be tied down by conventions or restrictive relationships. You need space to get on with your own thing, as well as a partner who shares your beliefs. George Eliot, the pseudonym of Mary Ann Evans, one of England's finest authors, broke a strict Victorian taboo by living openly, and happily, with a man to whom she was not married.

Sun in Scorpio with Venus in Capricorn

Björk	Richard Burton	Fyodor Dostoevsky
Indira Gandhi	George Gallup	Robert Kennedy

Your self-esteem is linked to the successful achievement of your goals, and you may need to be careful not to become so obsessive about moving towards them that you neglect other parts of your life. Richard Burton was frequently criticised for wasting his considerable talents on films that did not do them justice in order to achieve the fame and money that they offered – a fact that he never denied. The Icelandic singer Björk has chosen another path. After one uncomfortable experience in films, she has decided to devote herself, single-mindedly, to making music, saying that she has only another 50 years left and a lot of records to make. That's the Capricorn long-term perspective for you.

This kind of deliberate planning could come into your

relationships, too. It may take you some considerable time to make up your mind to commit, checking the situation out from every angle because you want it to last. You understand that, although marriages may be made in heaven, it takes time and effort on earth to keep them going. There may be an age or status difference between you and your lovers or partners. Partners who cause you difficulties, hardship or increased responsibilities may attract you like a magnet, as you love hard work and doing your duty. Alternatively, you may prefer a partner who is well-connected, well-heeled or established in their own field. With your appreciation of tradition, you have a love of history, antiques and old-world formality. Real happiness comes when you yourself find a respected position in the community in which you can make some substantial contribution, preferably one that will benefit posterity.

TEN

Famous Scorpio Birthdays

FIND OUT WHO SHARES YOUR MOON, MERCURY AND VENUS SIGNS AND ANY challenging Sun aspects and see what they have done with the material they were born with. Notice how often it is not just the personalities of the people themselves but the roles of actors, characters of authors and works of artists that reflect their astrological make-up. In reading standard biographies, I've been constantly astounded – and, of course, delighted – at how often phrases used to describe individuals could have been lifted straight from their astrological profiles. Check it out yourself!

A few people below have been given a choice of two Moons. This is because the Moon changed sign on the day that they were born and no birth time was available. You may be able to guess which one is correct if you read the descriptions of the Moon signs in Chapter Seven.

23 October
1844 Sarah Bernhardt, legendary actress, said to have had a thousand lovers
Sun aspects: Saturn, Pluto
Moon: Aries   Mercury: Libra   Venus: Virgo

24 October
1933 Ronald and Reginald Kray, London gangster twins, jailed for life for murder
Sun aspects: Saturn, Uranus, Pluto
Moon: Capricorn   Mercury: Scorpio   Venus: Sagittarius

25 October
1881 Pablo Picasso, one of the most influential artists of the twentieth century
Sun aspects: Saturn
Moon: Sagittarius   Mercury: Scorpio   Venus: Libra

26 October
1947 Hillary Clinton, US politician and wife of former US president Bill Clinton
Sun aspects: none
Moon: Pisces/Aries   Mercury: Scorpio   Venus: Scorpio

27 October
1939 John Cleese, actor, comedian and writer, *Fawlty Towers*, *Monty Python*
Sun aspects: Saturn, Pluto
Moon: Aries   Mercury: Scorpio   Venus: Scorpio

28 October
1955 Bill Gates, computer mogul and head of Microsoft
Sun aspects: Uranus, Neptune
Moon: Aries   Mercury: Libra   Venus: Scorpio

29 October
1740 James Boswell, man of letters and biographer of Dr Samuel Johnson
Sun aspects: Saturn, Pluto
Moon: Cancer/Leo   Mercury: Scorpio   Venus: Libra

30 October
1893 Charles Atlas, one-time weakling who marketed a body-building course
Sun aspects: Uranus
Moon: Cancer   Mercury: Scorpio   Venus: Sagittarius

31 October
1795 John Keats, Romantic poet, 'Ode to Autumn' and 'To a Nightingale'
Sun aspects: Neptune
Moon: Gemini/Cancer   Mercury: Sagittarius   Venus: Scorpio

1 November
1866 Cheiro, flamboyant Irish psychic and the first celebrity palmist
Sun aspects: Saturn, Pluto
Moon: Virgo   Mercury: Scorpio   Venus: Sagittarius

2 November
1755 Marie Antoinette, extravagant queen, guillotined in the French Revolution
Sun aspects: Neptune
Moon: Libra   Mercury: Sagittarius   Venus: Scorpio

3 November
1948 Lulu, Scottish singer, 'Shout'
Sun aspects: Pluto
Moon: Sagittarius   Mercury: Libra   Venus: Libra

4 November
1946 Laura Bush, wife of US President George W. Bush
Sun aspects: Saturn, Pluto
Moon: Pisces   Mercury: Sagittarius   Venus: Sagittarius

5 November
1913 Vivien Leigh, actress, Scarlett O'Hara in *Gone with the Wind*
Sun aspects: Uranus
Moon: Aquarius   Mercury: Sagittarius   Venus: Libra

6 November
1951 Nigel Havers, actor, *Chariots of Fire*
Sun aspects: Pluto
Moon: Aquarius   Mercury: Scorpio   Venus: Virgo

7 November
1867 Marie Curie, Polish physicist and Nobel Prize winner who isolated radium
Sun aspects: Pluto
Moon: Pisces   Mercury: Sagittarius   Venus: Scorpio

8 November
1900 Margaret Mitchell, author of *Gone With the Wind*
Sun aspects: none
Moon: Gemini   Mercury: Sagittarius   Venus: Libra

9 November
1961 Jill Dando, murdered TV presenter, *Crimewatch*
Sun aspects: Neptune
Moon: Scorpio/Sagittarius   Mercury: Libra   Venus: Libra

10 November
1483 Martin Luther, German priest who started the Reformation of the church
Sun aspects: none
Moon: Aries   Mercury: Sagittarius   Venus: Scorpio

11 November

1964 Calista Flockhart, ultra-thin actress and star of *Ally McBeal*
Sun aspects: Saturn, Neptune
Moon: Aquarius   Mercury: Sagittarius   Venus: Libra

12 November

1911 Chad Varah, founder of the Samaritans helpline for those in despair
Sun aspects: Saturn
Moon: Leo   Mercury: Sagittarius   Venus: Libra

13 November

1850 Robert Louis Stevenson, author, *Treasure Island, Dr Jekyll and Mr Hyde*
Sun aspects: none
Moon: Pisces   Mercury: Scorpio   Venus: Sagittarius

14 November

1948 Charles, Prince of Wales, heir to the British throne
Sun aspects: Pluto
Moon: Taurus   Mercury: Scorpio   Venus: Libra

15 November

1887 Georgia O'Keefe, US artist, best known for her outsize flowers
Sun aspects: Neptune
Moon: Scorpio/Sagittarius   Mercury: Scorpio Venus: Libra

16 November

1896 Sir Oswald Mosley, leading British fascist and Nazi supporter
Sun aspects: Saturn, Uranus
Moon: Aries   Mercury: Scorpio   Venus: Sagittarius

17 November
1942 Martin Scorsese, film director, *The Last Temptation of Christ*
Sun aspects: Uranus
Moon: Pisces   Mercury: Scorpio   Venus: Scorpio

18 November
1942 Linda Evans, actress, Krystle Carrington in 1980s soap opera *Dynasty*
Sun aspects: Uranus
Moon: Aries   Mercury: Scorpio   Venus: Scorpio

19 November
1917 Indira Gandhi, Indian prime minister, assassinated by her bodyguard
Sun aspects: Uranus
Moon: Capricorn   Mercury: Sagittarius   Venus: Capricorn

20 November
1908 Alistair Cooke, broadcaster of *Letter from America* for 58 years
Sun aspects: none
Moon: Libra   Mercury: Scorpio   Venus: Libra

21 November
1945 Goldie Hawn, shrewd dizzy blonde comedy actress, *Private Benjamin*
Sun aspects: none
Moon: Gemini   Mercury: Sagittarius   Venus: Scorpio

22 November

1819 George Eliot (Mary Ann Evans), English author, *Middlemarch*
Sun aspects: none
Moon: Capricorn   Mercury: Sagittarius   Venus: Sagittarius

Other Scorpio people mentioned in this book

Bryan Adams, singer, 'Everything I Do' ☆ David and Frederick Barclay, reclusive millionaire newspaper proprietors ☆ Christiaan Barnard, heart transplant pioneer ☆ Boris Becker, tennis champion ☆ Björk, singer, 'Play Dead' ☆ Benjamin Britten, composer, *Peter Grimes* ☆ Tina Brown, editor, *New Yorker* ☆ Richard Burton, actor, *Cleopatra* ☆ Albert Camus, author, *The Plague* ☆ Benvenuto Cellini, Italian sculptor, *Perseus with the Head of Medusa* ☆ Captain James Cook, English navigator who explored the Pacific ☆ Peter Cook, actor and co-founder of *Private Eye* magazine ☆ Nicholas Culpeper, English physician who created the basis for herbalism ☆ Alexandra David-Néel, French mystic and explorer, *My Journey to Lhasa* ☆ Robin Day, tough political interviewer with trademark bow-tie ☆ Bo Derek, actress and poster girl, *10* ☆ Leonardo Di Caprio, actor, *Titanic* ☆ Fyodor Dostoevsky, author, *Crime and Punishment* ☆ Richard Dreyfuss, actor, *Jaws* ☆ Adolf Driesch, experimental embryologist and parapsychologist ☆ Fenella Fielding, camp, sexy actress, *Drop Dead, Darling* ☆ Althea Flynt, porn magazine publisher, *Hustler* ☆ Jodie Foster, actress, *Taxi Driver* ☆ George Gallup, founder of first public opinion polls ☆ Charles de Gaulle, high-minded French president during and after the Second World War ☆ Terry Gilliam, film director and animator, *Monty Python* ☆ Whoopi Goldberg, actress, *Sister Act* ☆ Princess Grace, former actress who married Prince Rainer of Monaco, *High Society* ☆ Billy Graham, charismatic evangelist preacher ☆ Edmond Halley, astronomer and mathematician with a comet named after him ☆ Napoleon

Hill, inspirational writer, *Success Through a Positive Mental Attitude* ☆ Rock Hudson, actor, *Ice Station Zebra* ☆ Barbara Hutton, Woolworths heiress ☆ Lauren Hutton, supermodel, the original Revlon Charlie Girl ☆ Mahalia Jackson, gospel singer, 'Movin' On Up' ☆ Robert Kennedy, American politician assassinated in 1968 ☆ Billie Jean King, tennis champion ☆ Cleo Laine, jazz, pop and classical singer ☆ k.d. lang, singer, 'Miss Chatelaine' ☆ Viscount Linley, aristocratic furniture-maker ☆ René Magritte, Belgian Surrealist painter, *The Human Condition* ☆ Charles Manson, psychopathic murderer and cult leader ☆ Joseph McCarthy, American politician and inquisitor of supposed communists ☆ Joni Mitchell, folk singer, 'Clouds', 'Both Sides Now' ☆ Demi Moore, actress, *Indecent Proposal* ☆ President Nehru, Indian statesman allegedly the lover of Edwina, wife of Lord Mountbatten, last viceroy of India ☆ The Grand Duchess Olga of Russia, murdered after a year's imprisonment with her whole family in 1918 ☆ Tatum O'Neal, actress, *Paper Moon* ☆ William Penn, founder of the US state of Pennsylvania ☆ Sylvia Plath, poet, *The Bell Jar* ☆ Gordon Ramsay, celebrity chef ☆ Condoleeza Rice, US National Security Adviser ☆ Julia Roberts, actress, *Pretty Woman* ☆ Auguste Rodin, sculptor, *The Kiss*, *The Thinker* ☆ Jean Rook, unashamedly vulgar, 'Britain's bitchiest, best loved and loathed woman journalist' ☆ Erwin Rommel, German commander who tried to assassinate Hitler ☆ Jonathan Ross, radio and TV presenter ☆ Meg Ryan, actress, *Sleepless in Seattle* ☆ Winona Ryder, actress, *The Age of Innocence* ☆ Sir Jimmy Savile, DJ and TV presenter, *Top of the Pops* ☆ David Schwimmer, actor, Ross in *Friends* ☆ Sir George Trevelyan, New Age teacher ☆ Leon Trotsky, Russian revolutionary, assassinated with an ice pick ☆ Ted Turner, American entrepreneur once married to Jane Fonda ☆ The Walton sextuplets, the world's first surviving set of all-girl sextuplets

ELEVEN

Finding Your Sun, Moon, Mercury and Venus Signs

ALL OF THE ASTROLOGICAL DATA IN THIS BOOK WAS CALCULATED by Astrolabe, who also supply a wide range of astrological software. I am most grateful for their help and generosity.

ASTROLABE, PO Box 1750, Brewster, MA 02631, USA
www.alabe.com

PLEASE NOTE THAT ALL OF THE TIMES GIVEN ARE IN GREENWICH MEAN TIME (GMT). If you were born during British Summer Time (BST) you will need to subtract one hour from your birth time to convert it to GMT. If you were born outside of the British Isles, find the time zone of your place of birth and the number of hours it is different from GMT. Add difference in hours if you were born west of the UK, and subtract the difference if you were born east of the UK to convert your birth time to GMT.

Your Sun Sign

Check your year of birth, and if you were born between the dates and times given the Sun was in Scorpio when you were born – confirming that you're a Scorpio. If you were born before the time on the date that Scorpio begins in your year, you are a Libran. If you were born after the time on the date Scorpio ends in your year, you are a Sagittarius.

Your Moon Sign

The Moon changes sign every two and a half days. To find your Moon sign, first find your year of birth. You will notice that in each year box there are three columns.

The second column shows the day of the month that the Moon changed sign, while the first column gives the abbreviation for the sign that the Moon entered on that date.

In the middle column, the month has been omitted, so that the dates run from, for example, 23 to 31 (October) and then from 1 to 23 (November).

In the third column, after the star, the time that the Moon changed sign on that day is given.

Look down the middle column of your year box to find your date of birth. If your birth date is given, look to the third column to find the time that the Moon changed sign. If you were born after that time, your Moon sign is given in the first column next to your birth date. If you were born before that time, your Moon sign is the one above the one next to your birth date.

If your birth date is not given, find the closest date before it. The sign shown next to that date is your Moon sign.

If you were born on a day that the Moon changed signs and you do not know your time of birth, try out both of that day's Moon signs and feel which one fits you best.

The abbreviations for the signs are as follows:

Aries – Ari   Taurus – Tau   Gemini – Gem   Cancer – Can
Leo – Leo   Virgo – Vir   Libra – Lib   Scorpio – Sco
Sagittarius – Sag   Capricorn – Cap   Aquarius – Aqu   Pisces – Pis

Your Mercury Sign

Find your year of birth and then the column in which your birthday falls. Look up to the top of the column to find your Mercury sign. You will see that some dates appear twice. This is because Mercury changed sign that day. If your birthday falls on one of these dates, try out both Mercury signs and see which one fits you best. If you know your birth time, you can find out for sure which Mercury sign is yours on my website – www.janeridderpatrick.com.

Your Venus Sign

Find your year of birth and then the column in which your birthday falls. Look up to the top of the column to find your Venus sign. Some dates have two possible signs. That's because Venus changed signs that day. Try them both out and see which fits you best. If the year you are interested in doesn't appear in the tables, or you have Venus in the same sign as your Sun and want to know whether you have a morning or evening star Venus, you can find the information on my website – www.janeridderpatrick.com.

♏ Scorpio Sun Tables ☉

YEAR	SCORPIO BEGINS	SCORPIO ENDS
1930	24 Oct 03.25	23 Nov 00.34
1931	24 Oct 09.15	23 Nov 06.24
1932	23 Oct 15.03	22 Nov 12.10
1933	23 Oct 20.48	22 Nov 17.53
1934	24 Oct 02.36	22 Nov 23.44
1935	24 Oct 08.29	23 Nov 05.35
1936	23 Oct 14.18	22 Nov 11.25
1937	23 Oct 20.06	22 Nov 17.16
1938	24 Oct 01.53	22 Nov 23.06
1939	24 Oct 07.45	23 Nov 04.58
1940	23 Oct 13.39	22 Nov 10.48
1941	23 Oct 19.27	22 Nov 16.37
1942	24 Oct 01.15	22 Nov 22.30
1943	24 Oct 07.08	23 Nov 04.21
1944	23 Oct 12.55	22 Nov 10.07
1945	23 Oct 18.43	22 Nov 15.55
1946	24 Oct 00.34	22 Nov 21.46
1947	24 Oct 06.25	23 Nov 03.37
1948	23 Oct 12.18	22 Nov 09.28
1949	23 Oct 18.02	22 Nov 15.16
1950	23 Oct 23.44	22 Nov 21.02
1951	24 Oct 05.35	22 Nov 02.51
1952	23 Oct 11.22	22 Nov 08.35
1953	23 Oct 17.06	22 Nov 14.22
1954	23 Oct 22.56	22 Nov 20.14
1955	24 Oct 04.42	23 Nov 02.00
1956	23 Oct 10.34	22 Nov 07.49
1957	23 Oct 16.24	22 Nov 13.39
1958	23 Oct 22.11	22 Nov 19.29
1959	24 Oct 04.10	23 Nov 01.26
1960	23 Oct 10.01	22 Nov 07.18
1961	23 Oct 15.47	22 Nov 13.07
1962	23 Oct 21.39	22 Nov 19.01
1963	24 Oct 03.28	23 Nov 00.49

YEAR	SCORPIO BEGINS	SCORPIO ENDS
1964	23 Oct 09.20	22 Nov 06.38
1965	23 Oct 15.09	22 Nov 12.29
1966	23 Oct 20.50	22 Nov 18.14
1967	24 Oct 02.43	23 Nov 00.04
1968	23 Oct 08.29	22 Nov 05.48
1969	23 Oct 14.11	22 Nov 11.31
1970	23 Oct 20.04	22 Nov 17.24
1971	24 Oct 01.53	22 Nov 23.13
1972	23 Oct 07.41	22 Nov 05.02
1973	23 Oct 13.30	22 Nov 10.54
1974	23 Oct 19.10	22 Nov 16.38
1975	24 Oct 01.05	22 Nov 22.30
1976	23 Oct 12.40	22 Nov 10.07
1977	23 Oct 12.40	22 Nov 04.21
1978	23 Oct 18.37	22 Nov 16.04
1979	24 Oct 00.27	22 Nov 21.54
1980	23 Oct 06.17	22 Nov 03.41
1981	23 Oct 12.12	22 Nov 09.35
1982	23 Oct 17.57	22 Nov 15.23
1983	23 Oct 23.54	22 Nov 21.18
1984	23 Oct 05.45	22 Nov 03.10
1985	23 Oct 11.21	22 Nov 08.50
1986	23 Oct 17.14	22 Nov 20.29
1987	23 Oct 23.00	22 Nov 20.29
1988	23 Oct 04.44	22 Nov 02.11
1989	23 Oct 10.35	22 Nov 08.04
1990	23 Oct 16.13	22 Nov 13,46
1991	23 Oct 22.05	22 Nov 19.35
1992	23 Oct 03.57	22 Nov 01.25
1993	23 Oct 09.37	22 Nov 07.06
1994	23 Oct 15.35	22 Nov 13.05
1995	23 Oct 21.32	22 Nov 09.02
1996	23 Oct 03.18	22 Nov 00.49
1997	23 Oct 09.14	22 Nov 06.47
1998	23 Oct 14.58	22 Nov 12.34
1999	23 Oct 20.52	22 Nov 18.24
2000	23 Oct 02.47	22 Nov 00.19

♏ Scorpio – Finding Your Moon Sign ☽

1930		
Sag	24	*05:23
Cap	26	*12:27
Aqu	28	*22:54
Pis	31	*11:22
Ari	2	*23:33
Tau	5	*09:36
Gem	7	*16:58
Can	9	*22:04
Leo	12	*01:44
Vir	14	*04:41
Lib	16	*07:27
Sco	18	*10:36
Sag	20	*15:00

1931		
Ari	23	*20:20
Tau	26	*09:11
Gem	28	*20:47
Can	31	*06:26
Leo	2	*13:38
Vir	4	*18:07
Lib	6	*20:02
Sco	8	*20:20
Sag	10	*20:39
Cap	12	*22:53
Aqu	15	*04:40
Pis	17	*14:33
Ari	20	*03:08

1932		
Vir	25	*02:01
Lib	27	*05:15
Sco	29	*05:30
Sag	31	*04:40
Cap	2	*04:54
Aqu	4	*08:06
Pis	6	*15:07
Ari	9	*01:25
Tau	11	*13:33
Gem	14	*02:13
Can	16	*14:31
Leo	19	*01:34
Vir	21	*10:07

1933		
Cap	23	*16:13
Aqu	25	*18:48
Pis	27	*23:17
Ari	30	*05:40
Tau	1	*13:53
Gem	4	*00:02
Can	6	*12:05
Leo	9	*00:57
Vir	11	*12:22
Lib	13	*20:11
Sco	15	*23:50
Sag	18	*00:34
Cap	20	*00:24

1934		
Gem	24	*22:58
Can	27	*07:46
Leo	29	*19:42
Vir	1	*08:35
Lib	3	*19:40
Sco	6	*03:31
Sag	8	*08:32
Cap	10	*11:56
Aqu	12	*14:51
Pis	14	*17:56
Ari	16	*21:26
Tau	19	*01:47
Gem	21	*07:47

1935		
Lib	24	*16:31
Sco	27	*04:14
Sag	29	*14:16
Cap	31	*22:30
Aqu	3	*04:37
Pis	5	*08:19
Ari	7	*09:53
Tau	9	*10:29
Gem	11	*11:53
Can	13	*15:57
Leo	15	*23:51
Vir	18	*11:10
Lib	20	*23:51

1936		
Aqu	23	*12:58
Pis	25	*18:27
Ari	27	*20:08
Tau	29	*19:34
Gem	31	*18:49
Can	2	*20:00
Leo	5	*00:38
Vir	7	*09:00
Lib	9	*20:14
Sco	12	*08:51
Sag	14	*21:33
Cap	17	*09:19
Aqu	19	*19:10

1937		
Can	24	*05:46
Leo	26	*08:43
Vir	28	*14:02
Lib	30	*21:47
Sco	2	*07:48
Sag	4	*19:46
Cap	7	*08:49
Aqu	9	*21:18
Pis	12	*07:06
Ari	14	*12:58
Tau	16	*15:10
Gem	18	*15:09
Can	20	*14:47

1938		
Sco	23	*10:00
Sag	25	*17:54
Cap	28	*04:38
Aqu	30	*17:08
Pis	2	*05:08
Ari	4	*14:33
Tau	6	*20:39
Gem	9	*00:02
Can	11	*01:59
Leo	13	*03:49
Vir	15	*06:37
Lib	17	*11:03
Sco	19	*17:25

1939		
Pis	23	*00:05
Ari	25	*12:27
Tau	27	*23:08
Gem	30	*07:30
Can	1	*13:40
Leo	3	*18:01
Vir	5	*20:56
Lib	7	*23:03
Sco	10	*01:14
Sag	12	*04:41
Cap	14	*10:43
Aqu	16	*20:00
Pis	19	*08:00
Ari	21	*20:35

♏ Scorpio – Finding Your Moon Sign ☽

1940			1941			1942			1943			1944		
Leo	24	*04:50	Cap	24	*19:40	Tau	24	*03:52	Vir	23	*21:09	Aqu	24	*20:18
Vir	26	*09:08	Aqu	26	*23:03	Gem	26	*13:19	Lib	26	*08:37	Pis	26	*23:51
Lib	28	*10:35	Pis	29	*05:50	Can	29	*01:00	Sco	28	*17:14	Ari	29	*00:53
Sco	30	*10:24	Ari	31	*15:38	Leo	31	*13:47	Sag	30	*23:13	Tau	31	*00:45
Sag	1	*10:21	Tau	3	*03:19	Vir	3	*01:17	Cap	2	*03:36	Gem	2	*01:29
Cap	3	*12:23	Gem	5	*15:52	Lib	5	*09:20	Aqu	4	*07:09	Can	4	*05:04
Aqu	5	*18:03	Can	8	*04:25	Sco	7	*13:25	Pis	6	*10:15	Leo	6	*12:45
Pis	8	*03:46	Leo	10	*15:48	Sag	9	*14:46	Ari	8	*13:10	Vir	8	*23:59
Ari	10	*16:13	Vir	13	*00:27	Cap	11	*15:17	Tau	10	*16:32	Lib	11	*12:44
Tau	13	*05:12	Lib	15	*05:21	Aqu	13	*16:48	Gem	12	*21:32	Sco	14	*00:47
Gem	15	*17:00	Sco	17	*06:39	Pis	15	*20:28	Can	15	*05:22	Sag	16	*11:01
Can	18	*02:51	Sag	19	*05:53	Ari	18	*02:30	Leo	17	*16:27	Cap	18	*19:19
Leo	20	*10:37	Cap	21	*05:11	Tau	20	*10:38	Vir	20	*05:21	Aqu	21	*01:46

♏ Scorpio – Finding Your Moon Sign ☽

1945		
Gem	23	*08:50
Can	25	*10:12
Leo	27	*14:56
Vir	29	*23:12
Lib	1	*10:08
Sco	3	*22:29
Sag	6	*11:17
Cap	8	*23:34
Aqu	11	*09:57
Pis	13	*17:04
Ari	15	*20:23
Tau	17	*20:47
Gem	19	*20:02
Can	21	*20:14

1946		
Sco	24	*21:41
Sag	27	*09:03
Cap	29	*21:59
Aqu	1	*10:35
Pis	3	*20:30
Ari	6	*02:26
Tau	8	*04:48
Gem	10	*05:07
Can	12	*05:15
Leo	14	*06:52
Vir	16	*11:05
Lib	18	*18:12
Sco	21	*03:58

1947		
Pis	24	*17:45
Ari	27	*03:30
Tau	29	*10:15
Gem	31	*14:35
Can	2	*17:31
Leo	4	*20:03
Vir	6	*22:55
Lib	9	*02:42
Sco	11	*08:02
Sag	13	*15:33
Cap	16	*01:37
Aqu	18	*13:45
Pis	21	*02:15

1948		
Can	23	*05:21
Leo	25	*10:08
Vir	27	*12:52
Lib	29	*14:15
Sco	31	*15:31
Sag	2	*18:10
Cap	4	*23:40
Aqu	7	*08:41
Pis	9	*20:33
Ari	12	*09:11
Tau	14	*20:23
Gem	17	*05:01
Can	19	*11:10
Leo	21	*15:31

1949		
Sag	24	*00:08
Cap	26	*02:11
Aqu	28	*07:50
Pis	30	*17:21
Ari	2	*05:34
Tau	4	*18:36
Gem	7	*06:54
Can	9	*17:34
Leo	12	*01:59
Vir	14	*07:41
Lib	16	*10:34
Sco	18	*11:18
Sag	20	*11:15

103

♏ Scorpio – Finding Your Moon Sign ☽

1950		
Ari	23	*05:58
Tau	25	*17:02
Gem	28	*05:22
Can	30	*18:03
Leo	2	*05:37
Vir	4	*14:19
Lib	6	*19:09
Sco	8	*20:28
Sag	10	*19:51
Cap	12	*19:25
Aqu	14	*21:15
Pis	17	*02:39
Ari	19	*11:40
Tau	21	*23:07

1951		
Leo	23	*02:24
Vir	25	*14:00
Lib	27	*22:23
Sco	30	*03:08
Sag	1	*05:19
Cap	3	*06:39
Aqu	5	*08:43
Pis	7	*12:23
Ari	9	*17:52
Tau	12	*01:07
Gem	14	*10:15
Can	16	*21:27
Leo	19	*10:11
Vir	21	*22:34

1952		
Cap	23	*19:28
Aqu	25	*23:27
Pis	28	*02:22
Ari	30	*04:34
Tau	1	*06:58
Gem	3	*11:03
Can	5	*18:12
Leo	8	*04:56
Vir	10	*17:46
Lib	13	*05:57
Sco	15	*15:17
Sag	17	*21:32
Cap	20	*01:39

1953		
Gem	24	*15:04
Can	26	*18:23
Leo	29	*01:55
Vir	31	*13:04
Lib	3	*01:50
Sco	5	*14:11
Sag	8	*01:05
Cap	10	*10:17
Aqu	12	*17:30
Pis	14	*22:16
Ari	17	*00:34
Tau	19	*01:14
Gem	21	*01:55

1954		
Lib	24	*00:12
Sco	26	*12:10
Sag	29	*00:58
Cap	31	*13:35
Aqu	3	*00:20
Pis	5	*07:33
Ari	7	*10:41
Tau	9	*10:47
Gem	11	*09:50
Can	13	*10:00
Leo	15	*13:04
Vir	17	*19:52
Lib	20	*06:02

♏ Scorpio – Finding Your Moon Sign ☽

1955		
Aqu	23	*23:31
Pis	26	*09:35
Ari	28	*15:45
Tau	30	*18:29
Gem	1	*19:22
Can	3	*20:11
Leo	5	*22:20
Vir	8	*02:37
Lib	10	*09:15
Sco	12	*18:12
Sag	15	*05:17
Cap	17	*17:58
Aqu	20	*06:58

1956		
Can	24	*09:22
Leo	26	*12:26
Vir	28	*15:09
Lib	30	*18:09
Sco	1	*22:25
Sag	4	*04:56
Cap	6	*14:24
Aqu	9	*02:19
Pis	11	*14:50
Ari	14	*01:35
Tau	16	*09:11
Gem	18	*13:44
Can	20	*16:17

1957		
Sco	23	*05:30
Sag	25	*07:33
Cap	27	*12:42
Aqu	29	*21:32
Pis	1	*09:18
Ari	3	*21:59
Tau	6	*09:37
Gem	8	*19:08
Can	11	*02:22
Leo	13	*07:35
Vir	15	*11:06
Lib	17	*13:24
Sco	19	*15:17
Sag	21	*17:51

1958		
Ari	24	*19:10
Tau	27	*08:07
Gem	29	*20:49
Can	1	*08:08
Leo	3	*17:02
Vir	5	*22:44
Lib	8	*01:15
Sco	10	*01:29
Sag	12	*01:03
Cap	14	*01:55
Aqu	16	*05:52
Pis	18	*13:57
Ari	21	*01:28

1959		
Leo	24	*19:02
Vir	27	*03:47
Lib	29	*08:40
Sco	31	*10:13
Sag	2	*10:01
Cap	4	*10:05
Aqu	6	*12:15
Pis	8	*17:35
Ari	11	*02:10
Tau	13	*13:04
Gem	16	*01:16
Can	18	*13:56
Leo	21	*02:03

♏ Scorpio – Finding Your Moon Sign ☽

1960		
Cap	24	*22:28
Aqu	27	*00:57
Pis	29	*04:26
Ari	31	*09:11
Tau	2	*15:27
Gem	4	*23:45
Can	7	*10:26
Leo	9	*22:59
Vir	12	*11:23
Lib	14	*21:06
Sco	17	*02:52
Sag	19	*05:16
Cap	21	*06:01

1961		
Tau	23	*21:07
Gem	26	*00:25
Can	28	*07:03
Leo	30	*17:29
Vir	2	*06:17
Lib	4	*18:42
Sco	7	*04:39
Sag	9	*11:49
Cap	11	*16:59
Aqu	13	*20:58
Pis	16	*00:18
Ari	18	*03:10
Tau	20	*06:02

1962		
Vir	23	*02:31
Lib	25	*15:13
Sco	28	*03:48
Sag	30	*15:19
Cap	2	*01:16
Aqu	4	*09:01
Pis	6	*13:51
Ari	8	*15:44
Tau	10	*15:44
Gem	12	*15:43
Can	14	*17:48
Leo	16	*23:41
Vir	19	*09:33
Lib	21	*21:57

1963		
Cap	23	*03:20
Aqu	25	*14:18
Pis	27	*21:34
Ari	30	*00:38
Tau	1	*00:41
Gem	2	*23:48
Can	5	*00:09
Leo	7	*03:24
Vir	9	*10:14
Lib	11	*20:07
Sco	14	*07:56
Sag	16	*20:39
Cap	19	*09:22
Aqu	21	*20:50

1964		
Gem	23	*10:03
Can	25	*11:37
Leo	27	*14:14
Vir	29	*18:25
Lib	1	*00:24
Sco	3	*08:25
Sag	5	*18:43
Cap	8	*07:05
Aqu	10	*20:07
Pis	13	*07:27
Ari	15	*15:09
Tau	17	*18:56
Gem	19	*19:58
Can	21	*20:03

♏ Scorpio – Finding Your Moon Sign ☽

1965		
Sco	24	*12:32
Sag	26	*18:08
Cap	29	*03:05
Aqu	31	*14:49
Pis	3	*03:22
Ari	5	*14:20
Tau	7	*22:28
Gem	10	*03:53
Can	12	*07:29
Leo	14	*10:13
Vir	16	*12:54
Lib	18	*16:10
Sco	20	*20:37

1966		
Pis	23	*22:20
Ari	26	*11:02
Tau	28	*23:04
Gem	31	*09:27
Can	2	*17:42
Leo	4	*23:35
Vir	7	*03:09
Lib	9	*04:53
Sco	11	*05:53
Sag	13	*07:36
Cap	15	*11:37
Aqu	17	*19:03
Pis	20	*05:52

1967		
Can	23	*22:26
Leo	26	*07:39
Vir	28	*13:17
Lib	30	*15:30
Sco	1	*15:25
Sag	3	*14:51
Cap	5	*15:44
Aqu	7	*19:46
Pis	10	*03:43
Ari	12	*14:58
Tau	15	*03:52
Gem	17	*16:39
Can	20	*04:12

1968		
Sag	24	*00:32
Cap	26	*01:14
Aqu	28	*03:43
Pis	30	*08:54
Ari	1	*16:50
Tau	4	*03:01
Gem	6	*14:47
Can	9	*03:26
Leo	11	*15:44
Vir	14	*01:53
Lib	16	*08:25
Sco	18	*11:04
Sag	20	*11:03

1969		
Ari	23	*00:17
Tau	25	*05:32
Gem	27	*13:01
Can	29	*23:13
Leo	1	*11:34
Vir	3	*23:59
Lib	6	*09:57
Sco	8	*16:17
Sag	10	*19:29
Cap	12	*21:08
Aqu	14	*22:53
Pis	17	*01:52
Ari	19	*06:31
Tau	21	*12:52

♏ Scorpio – Finding Your Moon Sign ☽

1970		
Vir	24	*18:56
Lib	27	*07:36
Sco	29	*18:14
Sag	1	*02:23
Cap	3	*08:31
Aqu	5	*13:10
Pis	7	*16:32
Ari	9	*18:51
Tau	11	*20:50
Gem	13	*23:49
Can	16	*05:23
Leo	18	*14:36
Vir	21	*02:49

1971		
Cap	24	*16:04
Aqu	27	*00:09
Pis	29	*04:56
Ari	31	*06:25
Tau	2	*05:55
Gem	4	*05:27
Can	6	*07:15
Leo	8	*12:57
Vir	10	*22:44
Lib	13	*11:05
Sco	15	*23:49
Sag	18	*11:29
Cap	20	*21:35

1972		
Gem	24	*14:02
Can	26	*14:45
Leo	28	*18:14
Vir	31	*00:59
Lib	2	*10:27
Sco	4	*21:46
Sag	7	*10:16
Cap	9	*23:10
Aqu	12	*11:01
Pis	14	*19:55
Ari	17	*00:42
Tau	19	*01:51
Gem	21	*01:04

1973		
Lib	23	*15:28
Sco	25	*22:28
Sag	28	*07:57
Cap	30	*19:57
Aqu	2	*08:57
Pis	4	*20:25
Ari	7	*04:18
Tau	9	*08:24
Gem	11	*09:59
Can	13	*10:46
Leo	15	*12:20
Vir	17	*15:41
Lib	19	*21:16

1974		
Aqu	23	*03:20
Pis	25	*15:56
Ari	28	*03:12
Tau	30	*11:58
Gem	1	*18:22
Can	3	*23:00
Leo	6	*02:29
Vir	8	*05:17
Lib	10	*07:58
Sco	12	*11:23
Sag	14	*16:39
Cap	17	*00:42
Aqu	19	*11:39

♏ Scorpio – Finding Your Moon Sign ☽

1979		
Sag	23	*17:08
Cap	26	*00:10
Aqu	28	*05:16
Pis	30	*08:28
Ari	1	*10:08
Tau	3	*11:16
Gem	5	*13:26
Can	7	*18:23
Leo	10	*03:15
Vir	12	*15:20
Lib	15	*04:16
Sco	17	*15:28
Sag	19	*23:55

1978		
Leo	24	*00:03
Vir	26	*12:31
Lib	28	*22:49
Sco	31	*05:52
Sag	2	*10:02
Cap	4	*12:40
Aqu	6	*15:03
Pis	8	*18:05
Ari	10	*22:11
Tau	13	*03:35
Gem	15	*10:45
Can	17	*20:16
Leo	20	*08:08

1977		
Ari	24	*07:34
Tau	26	*16:53
Gem	29	*04:07
Can	31	*16:39
Leo	3	*05:02
Vir	5	*15:15
Lib	7	*21:49
Sco	10	*00:40
Sag	12	*01:03
Cap	14	*00:51
Aqu	16	*02:00
Pis	18	*05:58
Ari	20	*13:13

1976		
Sco	23	*05:16
Sag	25	*04:48
Cap	27	*05:55
Aqu	29	*10:06
Pis	31	*17:53
Ari	3	*04:45
Tau	5	*17:22
Gem	8	*06:20
Can	10	*18:27
Leo	13	*04:35
Vir	15	*11:44
Lib	17	*15:33
Sco	19	*16:31
Sag	21	*16:03

1975		
Can	25	*08:56
Leo	27	*15:18
Vir	29	*18:46
Lib	31	*19:54
Sco	2	*20:07
Sag	4	*21:10
Cap	7	*00:46
Aqu	9	*07:59
Pis	11	*18:41
Ari	14	*07:17
Tau	16	*19:37
Gem	19	*06:13
Can	21	*14:35

♏ Scorpio – Finding Your Moon Sign ☽

1980

Tau	23	*19:55
Gem	25	*19:17
Can	27	*21:01
Leo	30	*02:39
Vir	1	*12:19
Lib	4	*00:31
Sco	6	*13:18
Sag	9	*01:25
Cap	11	*12:14
Aqu	13	*21:09
Pis	16	*03:19
Ari	18	*06:21
Tau	20	*06:50

1981

Lib	25	*00:57
Sco	27	*11:38
Sag	29	*23:48
Cap	1	*12:45
Aqu	4	*00:49
Pis	6	*09:50
Ari	8	*14:37
Tau	10	*15:43
Gem	12	*14:59
Can	14	*14:37
Leo	16	*16:33
Vir	18	*21:53
Lib	21	*06:32

1982

Aqu	24	*21:35
Pis	27	*09:11
Ari	29	*17:24
Tau	31	*22:02
Gem	3	*00:22
Can	5	*01:58
Leo	7	*04:10
Vir	9	*07:40
Lib	11	*12:46
Sco	13	*19:42
Sag	16	*04:51
Cap	18	*16:21
Aqu	21	*05:20

1983

Gem	24	*09:09
Can	26	*14:46
Leo	28	*18:50
Vir	30	*21:32
Lib	1	*23:30
Sco	4	*01:53
Sag	6	*06:08
Cap	8	*13:32
Aqu	11	*00:10
Pis	13	*12:40
Ari	16	*00:35
Tau	18	*10:05
Gem	20	*16:44

1984

Sco	24	*10:08
Sag	26	*10:44
Cap	28	*14:05
Aqu	30	*21:14
Pis	2	*07:49
Ari	4	*20:20
Tau	7	*08:52
Gem	9	*20:09
Can	12	*05:31
Leo	14	*12:32
Vir	16	*17:07
Lib	18	*19:29
Sco	20	*20:30

♏ Scorpio – Finding Your Moon Sign ☽

1985		
Pis	23	*08:27
Ari	25	*18:47
Tau	28	*06:59
Gem	30	*19:58
Can	2	*08:30
Leo	4	*19:03
Vir	7	*02:17
Lib	9	*05:51
Sco	11	*06:30
Sag	13	*05:52
Cap	15	*05:53
Aqu	17	*08:26
Pis	19	*14:43

1986		
Can	23	*05:37
Leo	25	*18:02
Vir	28	*04:19
Lib	30	*11:03
Sco	1	*14:18
Sag	3	*15:18
Cap	5	*15:48
Aqu	7	*17:28
Pis	9	*21:30
Ari	12	*04:14
Tau	14	*13:24
Gem	17	*00:26
Can	19	*12:45

1987		
Sag	25	*00:56
Cap	27	*04:32
Aqu	29	*07:26
Pis	31	*10:19
Ari	2	*13:40
Tau	4	*18:01
Gem	7	*00:16
Can	9	*09:10
Leo	11	*20:45
Vir	14	*09:28
Lib	16	*20:47
Sco	19	*04:46
Sag	21	*09:15

1988		
Ari	23	*00:58
Tau	25	*01:22
Gem	27	*02:56
Can	29	*07:28
Leo	31	*16:03
Vir	3	*04:01
Lib	5	*17:03
Sco	8	*04:45
Sag	10	*14:04
Cap	12	*21:11
Aqu	15	*02:35
Pis	17	*06:33
Ari	19	*09:12
Tau	21	*11:01

1989		
Vir	24	*02:15
Lib	26	*14:11
Sco	29	*02:55
Sag	31	*15:22
Cap	3	*02:45
Aqu	5	*12:08
Pis	7	*18:24
Ari	9	*21:07
Tau	11	*21:08
Gem	13	*20:19
Can	15	*20:52
Leo	18	*00:47
Vir	20	*08:55

♏ Scorpio – Finding Your Moon Sign ☽

1990

Cap	24	*02:02
Aqu	26	*14:13
Pis	28	*23:20
Ari	31	*04:13
Tau	2	*05:31
Gem	4	*05:05
Can	6	*05:07
Leo	8	*07:24
Vir	10	*12:49
Lib	12	*21:08
Sco	15	*07:39
Sag	17	*19:39
Cap	20	*08:31

1991

Tau	23	*11:54
Gem	25	*15:08
Can	27	*17:36
Leo	29	*20:20
Vir	31	*23:46
Lib	3	*04:12
Sco	5	*10:09
Sag	7	*18:21
Cap	10	*05:16
Aqu	12	*18:06
Pis	15	*06:33
Ari	17	*16:06
Tau	19	*21:47

1992

Lib	23	*14:39
Sco	25	*16:04
Sag	27	*19:29
Cap	30	*02:18
Aqu	1	*12:43
Pis	4	*01:12
Ari	6	*13:18
Tau	8	*23:18
Gem	11	*06:49
Can	13	*12:18
Leo	15	*16:22
Vir	17	*19:27
Lib	19	*22:02

1993

Pis	24	*21:17
Ari	27	*09:39
Tau	29	*22:19
Gem	1	*10:12
Can	3	*20:23
Leo	6	*04:05
Vir	8	*08:46
Lib	10	*10:41
Sco	12	*10:59
Sag	14	*11:21
Cap	16	*13:35
Aqu	18	*19:08
Pis	21	*04:27

1994

Can	24	*22:14
Leo	27	*09:03
Vir	29	*16:20
Lib	31	*19:45
Sco	2	*20:19
Sag	4	*19:46
Cap	6	*20:02
Aqu	8	*22:49
Pis	11	*05:04
Ari	13	*14:44
Tau	16	*02:44
Gem	18	*15:41
Can	21	*04:20

♏ Scorpio – Finding Your Moon Sign ☽

1995			1996			1997			1998			1999			2000		
Sco	24	*04:06	Ari	24	*04:50	Leo	23	*05:10	Sag	23	*05:15	Tau	24	*19:24	Lib	24	*19:29
Sag	26	*05:56	Tau	26	*08:11	Vir	25	*16:59	Cap	25	*17:04	Gem	26	*19:33	Sco	27	*00:24
Cap	28	*07:14	Gem	28	*13:35	Lib	28	*06:04	Aqu	28	*02:43	Can	28	*20:09	Sag	29	*07:40
Aqu	30	*09:23	Can	30	*21:57	Sco	30	*18:15	Pis	30	*08:57	Leo	30	*22:48	Cap	31	*18:01
Pis	1	*13:18	Leo	2	*09:16	Sag	2	*04:26	Ari	1	*11:25	Vir	2	*04:07	Aqu	3	*06:40
Ari	3	*19:20	Vir	4	*21:56	Cap	4	*12:29	Tau	3	*11:11	Lib	4	*11:57	Pis	5	*19:12
Tau	6	*03:35	Lib	7	*09:27	Aqu	6	*18:33	Gem	5	*10:11	Sco	6	*21:46	Ari	8	*05:01
Gem	8	*13:54	Sco	9	*18:01	Pis	8	*22:33	Can	7	*10:40	Sag	9	*09:15	Tau	10	*11:10
Can	11	*01:56	Sag	11	*23:25	Ari	11	*00:42	Leo	9	*14:34	Cap	11	*22:00	Gem	12	*14:26
Leo	13	*14:36	Cap	14	*02:43	Tau	13	*01:44	Vir	11	*22:37	Aqu	14	*10:44	Can	14	*16:20
Vir	16	*02:01	Aqu	16	*05:13	Gem	15	*03:05	Lib	14	*09:57	Pis	16	*21:19	Leo	16	*18:18
Lib	18	*10:16	Pis	18	*07:59	Can	17	*06:32	Sco	16	*22:40	Ari	19	*03:56	Vir	18	*21:15
Sco	20	*14:39	Ari	20	*11:34	Leo	19	*13:39	Sag	19	*11:12	Tau	21	*06:25	Lib	21	*01:35
									Cap	21	*22:44						

♏ Scorpio Mercury Signs ☿

DATES	LIBRA	SCORPIO	SAGITTARIUS
1930	23 Oct–29 Oct	29 Oct–17 Nov	17 Nov–23 Nov
1931		23 Oct–10 Nov	10 Nov–23 Nov
1932		23 Oct–2 Nov	2 Nov–22 Nov
1933		23 Oct–30 Oct	30 Oct–16 Nov
		16 Nov–22 Nov	
1934		23 Oct–22 Nov	
1935	23 Oct–10 Nov	10 Nov–23 Nov	
1936	23 Oct–2 Nov	2 Nov–21 Nov	21 Nov–22 Nov
1937	23 Oct–26 Oct	26 Oct–13 Nov	13 Nov–22 Nov
1938		23 Oct–6 Nov	6 Nov–22 Nov
1939		23 Oct–1 Nov	1 Nov–23 Nov
1940		23 Oct–22 Nov	
1941	29 Oct–11 Nov	23 Oct–29 Oct	
		11 Nov–22 Nov	
1942	23 Oct–7 Nov	7 Nov–22 Nov	
1943	23 Oct–30 Oct	30 Oct–18 Nov	18 Nov–23 Nov
1944		23 Oct–10 Nov	10 Nov–22 Nov
1945		23 Oct–3 Nov	3 Nov–22 Nov
1946		23 Oct–30 Oct	30 Oct–20 Nov
		20 Nov–22 Nov	
1947		23 Oct–23 Nov	
1948	23 Oct–10 Nov	10 Nov–22 Nov	
1949	23 Oct–3 Nov	3 Nov–22 Nov	
1950	23 Oct–27 Oct	27 Oct–15 Nov	15 Nov–22 Nov
1951		23 Oct–8 Nov	8 Nov–23 Nov
1952		23 Oct–1 Nov	1 Nov–22 Nov
1953		23 Oct–31 Oct	31 Oct–6 Nov
		6 Nov–22 Nov	
1954	4 Nov–11 Nov	23 Oct–4 Nov	11 Nov–22 Nov
1955	23 Oct–8 Nov	8 Nov–23 Nov	
1956	23 Oct–31 Oct	31 Oct–18 Nov	18 Nov–22 Nov
1957	23 Oct	23 Oct–11 Nov	11 Nov–22 Nov
1958		23 Oct–5 Nov	5 Nov–22 Nov
1959		23 Oct–31 Oct	31 Oct–23 Nov
1960		23 Oct–22 Nov	
1961	23 Oct–10 Nov	10 Nov–22 Nov	
1962		23 Oct–22 Nov	
1963	23 Oct–28 Oct	28 Oct–16 Nov	16 Nov–23 Nov
1964		23 Oct–8 Nov	8 Nov–22 Nov
1965		23 Oct–2 Nov	2 Nov–22 Nov

DATES	LIBRA	SCORPIO	SAGITTARIUS
1966		23 Oct–30 Oct 13 Nov–22 Nov	30 Oct–13 Nov
1967		23 Oct–23 Nov	
1968	23 Oct–8 Nov	8 Nov–22 Nov	
1969	23 Oct–1 Nov	1 Nov–20 Nov	20 Nov–22 Nov
1970	23 Oct–25 Oct	25 Oct–13 Nov	13 Nov–22 Nov
1971		23 Oct–6 Nov	6 Nov–22 Nov
1972		23 Oct–30 Oct	30 Oct–22 Nov
1973		23 Oct–22 Nov	
1974	26 Oct–11 Nov	23 Oct–26 Oct 11 Nov–22 Nov	
1975	23 Oct–6 Nov	6 Nov–22 Nov	
1976	23 Oct–29 Oct	29 Oct–16 Nov	16 Nov–22 Nov
1977		23 Oct–9 Nov	9 Nov–22 Nov
1978		23 Oct–3 Nov	3 Nov–22 Nov
1979		23 Oct–30 Oct 18 Nov–22 Nov	30 Oct–18 Nov
1980		23 Oct–22 Nov	
1981	23 Oct–9 Nov	9 Nov–22 Nov	
1982	23 Oct–3 Nov	3 Nov–22 Nov	22 Nov
1983	23 Oct–26 Oct	26 Oct–14 Nov	14 Nov–22 Nov
1984		23 Oct–6 Nov	6 Nov–22 Nov
1985		23 Oct–31 Oct	31 Oct–22 Nov
1986		23 Oct–22 Nov	
1987	1 Nov–11 Nov	23 Oct–1 Nov 11 Nov–22 Nov	
1988	23 Oct–6 Nov	6 Nov–22 Nov	
1989	23 Oct–30 Oct	30 Oct–18 Nov	18 Nov–22 Nov
1990		23 Oct–11 Nov	11 Nov–22 Nov
1991		23 Oct–4 Nov	4 Nov–22 Nov
1992		23 Oct–29 Oct 21 Nov–22 Nov	29 Oct–21 Nov
1993		23 Oct–22 Nov	
1994	23 Oct–10 Nov	10 Nov–22 Nov	
1995	23 Oct–4 Nov	4 Nov–22 Nov	
1996	23 Oct–27 Oct	27 Oct–14 Nov	14 Nov–22 Nov
1997		23 Oct–7 Nov	7 Nov–22 Nov
1998		23 Oct–1 Nov	1 Nov–22 Nov
1999		23 Oct–30 Oct 9 Nov–22 Nov	30 Oct–9 Nov
2000	7 Nov–8 Nov	23 Oct–7 Nov 8 Nov–22 Nov	

♏ Scorpio Venus Signs ♀

YEAR	VIRGO	LIBRA	SCORPIO	SAGITTARIUS	CAPRICORN
1930			22 Nov–23 Nov	23 Oct–22 Nov	
1931			23 Oct–7 Nov	7 Nov–23 Nov	
1932	23 Oct–2 Nov	2 Nov–22 Nov			6 Nov–22 Nov
1933			29 Oct–22 Nov	23 Oct–6 Nov	
1934					
1935	23 Oct–9 Nov	23 Oct–29 Oct			16 Nov–22 Nov
1936		9 Nov–23 Nov	23 Oct	23 Oct–16 Nov	
1937			12 Nov–22 Nov	23 Oct–15 Nov	15 Nov–22 Nov
1938		23 Oct–12 Nov		23 Oct–15 Nov	15 Nov–22 Nov
1939			23 Oct–7 Nov	7 Nov–23 Nov	
1940	23 Oct–1 Nov	1 Nov–22 Nov			
1941					
1942		23 Oct–28 Oct	28 Oct–22 Nov	23 Oct–6 Nov	6 Nov–22 Nov
1943	23 Oct–9 Nov	9 Nov–23 Nov		22 Nov	
1944				23 Oct–16 Nov	16 Nov–22 Nov
1945		23 Oct–12 Nov	12 Nov–22 Nov		
1946			2 Nov–22 Nov	23 Oct–2 Nov	
1947			23 Oct–6 Nov	6 Nov–23 Nov	
1948			23 Oct–1 Nov	1 Nov–22 Nov	
1949				23 Oct–6 Nov	6 Nov–22 Nov
1950		23 Oct–28 Oct	28 Oct–22 Nov		
1951	23 Oct–9 Nov	9 Nov–23 Nov			
1952				23 Oct–15 Nov	15 Nov–22 Nov

YEAR	VIRGO	LIBRA	SCORPIO	SAGITTARIUS	CAPRICORN
1953		23 Oct–11 Nov	11 Nov–22 Nov	23 Oct–27 Oct	27 Oct–22 Nov
1954			23 Oct	6 Nov–23 Nov	
1955			23 Oct–6 Nov		
1956	23 Oct–31 Oct	31 Oct–22 Nov			5 Nov–22 Nov
1957					
1958		23 Oct–27 Oct	27 Oct–22 Nov	23 Oct–5 Nov	
1959	23 Oct–9 Nov	9 Nov–23 Nov			
1960				23 Oct–15 Nov	15 Nov–22 Nov
1961		23 Oct–11 Nov	11 Nov–22 Nov		
1962			23 Oct–22 Nov		
1963			23 Oct–5 Nov	5 Nov–23 Nov	
1964	23 Oct–31 Oct	31 Oct–22 Nov			
1965					5 Nov–22 Nov
1966		23 Oct–27 Oct	27 Oct–20 Nov	23 Oct–5 Nov	
1967	23 Oct–9 Nov	9 Nov–23 Nov		20 Nov–22 Nov	
1968				23 Oct–14 Nov	14 Nov–22 Nov
1969		23 Oct–10 Nov	10 Nov–22 Nov		
1970			23 Oct–22 Nov		
1971			23 Oct–5 Nov	5 Nov–22 Nov	
1972	23 Oct–30 Oct	30 Oct–22 Nov			
1973					
1974		23 Oct–26 Oct	26 Oct–19 Nov	23 Oct–5 Nov	5 Nov–22 Nov
1975	23 Oct–9 Nov	9 Nov–22 Nov		19 Nov–22 Nov	
1976					
1977		23 Oct–10 Nov	10 Nov–22 Nov	23 Oct–14 Nov	14 Nov–22 Nov

YEAR	VIRGO	LIBRA	SCORPIO	SAGITTARIUS	CAPRICORN
1978			23 Oct–22 Nov	4 Nov–22 Nov	
1979			23 Oct–4 Nov		
1980	23 Oct–30 Oct	30 Oct–22 Nov			5 Nov–22 Nov
1981					
1982		23 Oct–26 Oct	26 Oct–18 Nov	23 Oct–5 Nov	
1983	23 Oct–9 Nov	9 Nov–22 Nov		18 Nov–22 Nov	
1984				23 Oct–13 Nov	13 Nov–22 Nov
1985				23 Oct–9 Nov	9 Nov–22 Nov
1986		23 Oct–3 Nov	23 Oct–22 Nov		
1987		29 Oct–22 Nov	3 Nov–22 Nov		
1988	23 Oct–29 Oct				
1989		23 Oct–25 Oct	25 Oct–18 Nov	23 Oct–5 Nov	5 Nov–22 Nov
1990		9 Nov–22 Nov		18 Nov–22 Nov	
1991	23 Oct–9 Nov			23 Oct–13 Nov	13 Nov–22 Nov
1992		23 Oct–9 Nov	9 Nov–22 Nov		
1993			23 Oct–22 Nov		
1994			23 Oct–3 Nov	3 Nov–22 Nov	
1995					
1996	23 Oct–29 Oct	29 Oct–22 Nov			
1997			24 Oct–17 Nov	23 Oct–5 Nov	5 Nov–22 Nov
1998	23 Oct–24 Oct	23 Oct–24 Oct		17 Nov–22 Nov	
1999	23 Oct–9 Nov	9 Nov–22 Nov		13 Nov–22 Nov	
2000			23 Oct–13 Nov		

The Scorpio Workbook

There are no right or wrong answers in this chapter. Its aim is to help you assess how you are doing with your life – in YOUR estimation – and to make the material of this book more personal and, I hope, more helpful for you.

1. The Scorpio in You

Which of the following Scorpio characteristics do you recognise in yourself?

resourceful	courageous	private
dignified	heroic	incorruptible
determined	purposeful	loyal
transformative	passionate	powerful

2. In which situations do you find yourself acting like this?

_____

_____

3. When you are feeling vulnerable, you may show some of the less constructive Scorpio traits. Do you recognise yourself in any of the following?

vindictive	paranoid	obsessive
intimidating	exploiting	cruel
ruthless	controlling	withholding

What kind of situations trigger off this behaviour and what do you think might help you, in these situations, to respond more positively?

_____

_____

4. You and Your Roles

a) Where, if anywhere, in your life do you play the role of Survivor?

_____

_____

b) Whom, or what, do you survive?

_____

_____

5. Do you play any of the following roles – in the literal or broad sense – in any part of your life? If not, would you like to? What might be your first step towards doing so?

Investigator   Power Broker   Taboo Breaker
Transformer   Whistle-blower   Midwife

_____

_____

6. Sun Aspects

If any of the following planets aspects your Sun, add each of the keywords for that planet to complete the following sentences. Which phrases ring true for you?

I am _____

My father is _____

My job requires that I am _____

Saturn Words (Use only if your Sun is aspected by Saturn)

ambitious	controlling	judgmental	mature
serious	strict	traditional	bureaucratic
cautious	committed	hard-working	disciplined
depressive	responsible	status-seeking	limiting

Uranus Words (Use only if your Sun is aspected by Uranus)

freedom-loving	progressive	rebellious	shocking
scientific	cutting-edge	detached	contrary
friendly	disruptive	eccentric	humanitarian
innovative	nonconformist	unconventional	exciting

Neptune Words (Use only if your Sun is aspected by Neptune)

sensitive	idealistic	artistic	impressionable
disappointing	impractical	escapist	self-sacrificing
spiritual	unrealistic	dreamy	glamorous
dependent	deceptive	rescuing	blissful

Pluto Words (Use only if your Sun is aspected by Pluto)

powerful	single-minded	intense	extreme
secretive	rotten	passionate	mysterious
investigative	uncompromising	ruthless	wealthy
abusive	regenerative	associated with sex, birth or death	

a) If one or more negative words describe you or your job, how might you turn that quality into something more positive or satisfying?

_____

_____

7. The Moon and You

Below are brief lists of what the Moon needs, in the various elements, to feel secure and satisfied. First find your Moon element, then estimate how much of each of the following you are expressing and receiving in your life, especially at home and in your relationships, on a scale of 0 to 5 where 0 = none and 5 = plenty.

FIRE MOONS — Aries, Leo, Sagittarius

attention	action	drama
recognition	self-expression	spontaneity
enthusiasm	adventure	leadership

EARTH MOONS — Taurus, Virgo, Capricorn

stability	orderly routine	sensual pleasures
material security	a sense of rootedness	control over your home life
regular body care	practical achievements	pleasurable practical tasks

AIR MOONS — Gemini, Libra, Aquarius

mental rapport	stimulating ideas	emotional space
friendship	social justice	interesting conversations
fairness	socialising	freedom to circulate

WATER MOONS — Cancer, Scorpio, Pisces

intimacy	a sense of belonging	emotional rapport
emotional safety	respect for your feelings	time and space to retreat
acceptance	cherishing and being cherished	warmth and comfort

a) Do you feel your Moon is being 'fed' enough?
yes _____ no _____

b) How might you satisfy your Moon needs even better?

_____

_____

8. You and Your Mercury

As a Scorpio, your Mercury can only be in Libra, Scorpio or Sagittarius. Below are some of the ways and situations in which Mercury in each of the elements might learn and communicate effectively. First find your Mercury sign then circle the words you think apply to you.

Mercury in Fire (Sagittarius)

| action | imagination | identifying with the subject matter |
| excitement | drama | playing with possibilities |

Mercury in Earth (As a Scorpio you can never have Mercury in an earth sign; the words are included here for completeness)

| time-tested methods | useful facts | well-structured information |
| 'how to' instructions | demonstrations | hands-on experience |

Mercury in Air (Libra)

| facts arranged in categories | logic | demonstrable connections |
| rational arguments | theories | debate and sharing of ideas |

Mercury in Water (Scorpio)

| pictures and images | charged atmospheres | feeling-linked information |
| intuitive understanding | emotional rapport | being shown personally |

a) This game with Mercury can be done with a friend or on

your own. Skim through a magazine until you find a picture that interests you. Then describe the picture – to your friend, or in writing or on tape. Notice what you emphasise and the kind of words you use. Now try to describe it using the language and emphasis of each of the other Mercury modes. How easy did you find that? Identifying the preferred Mercury style of others and using that style yourself can lead to improved communication all round.

9. Your Venus Values

Below are lists of qualities and situations that your Venus sign might enjoy. Assess on a scale of 0 to 5 how much your Venus desires and pleasures are met and expressed in your life. 0 = not at all, 5 = fully.

Venus in Virgo

You will activate your Venus through anything that engages your powers of discrimination, for example:

restoring order   improving efficiency   using your skills
purifying your mind,   being of service   quality work
body or environment

Venus in Libra

You will activate your Venus through anything cultured, balanced and fair, for example:

harmonious   elegant surroundings   dressing well
relationships
courteous manners   artistic pursuits   political justice

Venus in Scorpio

You will activate your Venus through anything that allows you to penetrate to the heart of life's mysteries, for example:

survival situations	money, power and sex	investigating secrets
transformative experiences	recycling	intense relationships

Venus in Sagittarius

You will activate your Venus through following your adventurous spirit, opening up new frontiers and sharing your enthusiasm with others, for example:

travelling	sport	searching for the meaning of life
teaching or preaching	inspiring others	publishing or broadcasting

Venus in Capricorn

You will activate your Venus through anything that makes you feel a respected member of the community, for example:

doing your duty	upholding tradition	working towards goals
achieving ambitions	heading a dynasty	acquiring social status

a) How, and where, might you have more fun and pleasure by bringing more of what your Venus sign loves into your life?

b) Make a note here of the kind of gifts your Venus sign would love to receive. Then go on and spoil yourself . . .

Resources

Finding an Astrologer

I'm often asked what is the best way to find a reputable astrologer. Personal recommendation by someone whose judgement you trust is by far the best way. Ideally, the astrologer should also be endorsed by a reputable organisation whose members adhere to a strict code of ethics, which guarantees confidentiality and professional conduct.

Contact Addresses

Association of Professional Astrologers International
www.professionalastrologers.org

APAI members adhere to a strict code of professional ethics.

Astrological Association of Great Britain
www.astrologicalassociation.co.uk

The main body for astrology in the UK, with links to similar organisations throughout the world.

Faculty of Astrological Studies
www.astrology.org.uk

The teaching body internationally recognised for excellence in astrological education at all levels.

Jane Ridder-Patrick
www.janeridderpatrick.com

Your Scorpio Friends

You can keep a record of Scorpios you know here, with the
page numbers of where to find their descriptions handy for
future reference.

Name _____   Date of Birth _____

Aspects★	None	Saturn	Uranus	Neptune	Pluto
Moon Sign _____				p _____	
Mercury Sign _____				p _____	
Venus Sign _____				p _____	

Name _____   Date of Birth _____

Aspects★	None	Saturn	Uranus	Neptune	Pluto
Moon Sign _____				p _____	
Mercury Sign _____				p _____	
Venus Sign _____				p _____	

Name _____   Date of Birth _____

Aspects★	None	Saturn	Uranus	Neptune	Pluto
Moon Sign _____				p _____	
Mercury Sign _____				p _____	
Venus Sign _____				p _____	

Name _____   Date of Birth _____

Aspects★	None	Saturn	Uranus	Neptune	Pluto
Moon Sign _____				p _____	
Mercury Sign _____				p _____	
Venus Sign _____				p _____	

★ Circle where applicable

Sign Summaries

SIGN	GLYPH	APPROX DATES	SYMBOL	ROLE	ELEMENT	QUALITY	PLANET	GLYPH	KEYWORD
1. Aries	♈	21/3 – 19/4	Ram	Hero	Fire	Cardinal	Mars	♂	Assertiveness
2. Taurus	♉	20/4 – 20/5	Bull	Steward	Earth	Fixed	Venus	♀	Stability
3. Gemini	♊	21/5 – 21/6	Twins	Go-Between	Air	Mutable	Mercury	☿	Communication
4. Cancer	♋	22/6 – 22/7	Crab	Caretaker	Water	Cardinal	Moon	☽	Nurture
5. Leo	♌	23/7 – 22/8	Lion	Performer	Fire	Fixed	Sun	☉	Glory
6. Virgo	♍	23/8 – 22/9	Maiden	Craftworker	Earth	Mutable	Mercury	☿	Skill
7. Libra	♎	23/9 – 22/10	Scales	Architect	Air	Cardinal	Venus	♀	Balance
8. Scorpio	♏	23/10 – 23/11	Scorpion	Survivor	Water	Fixed	Pluto	♇	Transformation
9. Sagittarius	♐	22/11 – 21/12	Archer	Adventurer	Fire	Mutable	Jupiter	♃	Wisdom
10. Capricorn	♑	22/12 – 19/1	Goat	Manager	Earth	Cardinal	Saturn	♄	Responsibility
11. Aquarius	♒	20/1 – 19/2	Waterbearer	Scientist	Air	Fixed	Uranus	♅	Progress
12. Pisces	♓	20/2 – 20/3	Fishes	Dreamer	Water	Mutable	Neptune	♆	Universality